*Losing
Malcolm*

Losing Malcolm

A Mother's Journey Through Grief

For Paul —
with hope and heart

and Macs.

Carol Henderson

University Press of Mississippi
Jackson

Carol Henderson
July 2006

www.upress.state.ms.us

Manufactured in the United States of America

09   08   07   06   05   04   03   02   01   4   3   2   1
∞
Library of Congress Cataloging-in-Publication Data

Henderson, Carol.
Losing Malcolm : a mother's journey through grief / Carol
Henderson.
p.   cm.
ISBN 1-57806-339-6 (cloth : alk. paper)
1. Grief.   2. Bereavement — Psychological aspects.
3. Infants — Death — Psychological aspects.
4. Loss (Psychology)   I. Title.
BF575.G7 H46 2001
155.9'37'092 — dc21
[B]
00-064670

British Library Cataloging-in-Publication Data available

For my parents

Grief fills the room of my absent child,
lies in his bed, walks up and down with me.

Shakespeare, from "King John"

I wanted to fill the house
with umbels of Queen Anne's lace.
Corbel and lintel, shutter and fanlight,
this house was yours.

Sue Standing, from "Gravida"

Contents

Preface

Give sorrow words; the grief that does not speak
Whispers the o'er fraught heart, and bids it break.

Shakespeare, *Macbeth*

A few years ago I began to organize a group of my news-paper columns into what I hoped would someday be a book. Parenting was my beat — the calamities, challenges, and joys involved in rearing children.

My writing was anecdotal and, I hoped, light-hearted and accessible. I didn't have enough material for a book yet, so I decided to write more essays in my spare time. But with two energetic young daughters, writing dead-lines, a busy husband, demanding pets, and a household to manage, I was finding little free time for extra projects.

Quite unexpectedly, a chunk of time opened up. One of our dogs had been a recent acquisition from the pound. Rosie was a nervous, needy puppy who awoke each day before dawn and, despite the companionship of our other dog, whimpered desperately to be let out of the kitchen. Fearing Rosie's lamentations would wake the children, I stumbled into the dark kitchen, morning after morning, groggy and half asleep, to sit with her and keep her quiet.

One morning, on my way to the kitchen, I reached for my laptop. With Rosie curled at my feet, I wrote for a solid hour at the kitchen table before the rest of the family woke up.

These early morning writing sessions became a red-eyed ritual. Maybe it was the wee small hours, maybe my semi-alert state, but what emerged over the next few months was not at all the breezy sort of material I had hoped would come. Instead, I found myself writing about the life and death of our infant son Malcolm, who had lived for six weeks, two years before our first daughter Olivia was born. His harrowing story — and my painful passage through grief — loomed up and demanded space on the page.

A cardboard box in our attic contained the letters and cards we had received about Malcolm from friends and relatives. I reread each piece of correspondence and let myself study the few snapshots we had taken of our son. I held his tiny plastic ID bracelets, the ones he had worn around his wrists in the hospitals he had passed through. And I pored over the journals I had kept during Malcolm's brief life and the years immediately following it.

I read books and articles on grief. One researcher who analyzed nineteenth-century diaries found that, although most people recover from acute grief within a few years, active grieving continues to follow a person through life. The anguish, when it comes, is as deep and as powerful as in the beginning, but doesn't last as long, and eventually becomes less frequent.

All too well, I know this to be true.

It is my hope that readers who are suffering from a loss — of a child, a pregnancy, a parent, or a friend — will find some comfort in these pages. *Someone else has been there.* Often just to be able to share that knowledge enhances the healing process. This then is the book I wish I could have read when Malcolm died. I might have felt a little less crazy, a little less frightened, and a little less isolated.

There is practical advice here. I would be overjoyed, for example, if readers choose to do what finally and ultimately preserved my sanity — keep their own journals. I would also hope that after reading this book, parents struggling with the procedural jungle of the modern-day hospital will feel empowered to be aggressive advocates for their loved ones. Finally, for those fortunate enough never to have experienced devastating grief, I hope *Losing Malcolm* will offer meaningful insights into how to respond to others who have.

Losing
Malcolm

Torn Hearts

Weeks go by.
Slowly night comes.

Tomas Transtromer, "Lamento"

Fear

That morning will be etched in my mind forever. It was when my world, the one I had so vigilantly constructed, began to unravel.

"How's everything going?" the pediatrician asked, peering first at the newborn in my arms and then at my face. He hadn't seen us since Malcolm's birth by cesarean three days earlier, when he had declared my son "perfect." Now, in my postpartum daze, I barely recognized this stocky man with his outdoorsman's complexion and hair the color of sand.

"We're doing all right," I said, in a whisper. I didn't want to disturb Malcolm, who seemed deep in sleep. His small chest heaved irregularly, like the flank of a dreaming dog when it's hot on the chase.

Having heard through the nurses' grapevine that my doctor was back from his fishing trip and making morning rounds, I had brushed my hair and raised the angle of the uncomfortable motorized bed, trying to pretend it was a chaise longue and not a modern-day Marat-Sade torture machine.

"The nurses tell me you've been up and around quite a bit," the doctor said.

I was proud of my swift convalescence, after forty sleepless hours of back labor that never progressed beyond the "she's-still-two-centimeters-dilated" stage. The morning after the cesarean, one of the nurses had catapulted me out of bed and ordered me to walk, if I wanted a successful recovery. Since then, I had made countless tummy-clutching shuffles up and down the hall, pushing Malcolm in his rolling steel crib.

"We've already taken a walk this morning," I said.

"Well, don't overdo it on the exercise," the doctor said, wagging his index finger at me. "There's no need to be a supermom!"

I could feel my cheeks redden at the scolding, but not being one to stick up for myself, I tried to think of something neutral, even amiable, to say in response. After all, this guy was going to be our pediatrician, probably for years. But my brain seemed empty, mindless. I had heard that this happened, that once a woman starting having babies her IQ seeped out in the breast milk.

I had an important question about something, but I couldn't remember what it was. Lab-coat-induced amnesia is what I called my condition. A drop of sweat rolled down my rib cage. I knew people who were phobic about heights or tunnels or snakes. For me, it was doctors. No amount of small talk or deep breathing had ever helped me over this fear of "the medicine man," this powerful icon capable of foreseeing the future. Already, my tongue was as dry as sandpaper, my palms moist, and my underarms leaking.

My mind froze as I gazed down at Malcolm. His lips were pinched together and making a cute sucking motion in his sleep. That was it, that was my question! Breast feeding.

"We're having a little trouble with feedings," I said.

"What kind of trouble?" The doctor rubbed the flat part of his stethoscope against his lab coat and pulled a plastic chair close to the bed.

"He can't seem to keep much food down."

I waited for a comment. Instead, the doctor rummaged through the big white pocket of his coat and produced swabs, wooden tongue depressors, cellophane bags. He didn't speak, so I kept talking.

"The nurses say he's lazy at the breast and I should flick him on his heel to wake him up." The doctor didn't look at me. "Or else change his diaper. He wakes up, but as soon as he starts sucking he falls asleep again. Or spits up."

Still no response. My lower lip cracked and I could taste blood. Why was the doctor so silent? Because I was talking about breast feeding and the tricks of nurses? Did he think this was all beneath concern or just plain idiotic?

He placed the ends of the stethoscope in his ears, gently unwrapped the cotton swaddling blanket, the way you do tissue paper in a box to find the gift inside, and placed the business end on Malcolm's chest. At least he wasn't the rough type. I could smell the natural oils in the man's hair, just beneath the Old Spice or whatever cologne he wore. He listened intently, then moved the scope to another spot.

Malcolm opened his eyes and looked at the man's face. Instantly, his small brow knitted and his lips pushed out in a pout. Apparently he didn't like doctors either. At three days old, he was already such a pensive boy and so quiet. My husband Bill and I had agreed that, so far anyway, having a baby was no problem. Malcolm seemed only to want to lie in his isolette or in my arms, motionless and soundless, except for the little grunting noises he made as he breathed.

The doctor moved the stethoscope several times, as though inching a checker across a tiny game board. He turned Malcolm over in my arms and listened to his back, first on the left side, then on the right.

I recalled how my OB-GYN had monitored Malcolm's heart when it was still hidden under layers of my own flesh. I had heard it too, a steady, fast, whooshing, like a wild bird's pulse. I couldn't hold my son in my arms then, look at his full cheeks, or stroke his strawberry blond hair, but on some primordial level I already knew him. I savored his hiccups and kicks and the calm in my womb when he rested. I sensed that he listened to me when I talked and sang to him. Now that Malcolm was on the outside, I still felt we were tethered by a sturdy cord, like the umbilical, only now it was invisible.

"Your baby has a heart murmur," the doctor said, pulling the tips of the stethoscope out of his ears and, for the first time, looking me in the eye. He took Malcolm out of my arms, wrapped him in his blanket, and lay him on his side in his rolling crib, as though he were damaged goods, not to be handled.

"He needs to be seen by a specialist immediately. I've got to try to catch the cardiologist before she leaves home."

And he vanished.

I motored myself upward in the bed, picked up the phone receiver on the tray table, and dialed home. My own heartbeat thundered in my ear.

After several rings, Bill picked up. "Malcolm has a heart murmur," I said, my throat as stiff as taffy. I could barely push the words out. "A specialist is coming."

"I'll be right there," Bill said after a pause and hung up. I put the receiver down and stared at the phone. It was unlike him to be so abrupt. Usually, when I was upset, I could count on Bill for something soothing like, "Don't worry, honey, I'm sure it's nothing serious." Almost immediately, I would feel the beginning of relief. He hadn't done that this time.

I looked out the window. The sunny dawn had been blotted out by one of those swiftly unfurling coastal fogs common to this part of New England, turning my hospital view from dappled Impressionism into a solid gray rectangle. There was a buzzing in the electric clock on the opposite wall and I wondered how I could have spent so many fitful hours in this room without hearing it until now. I watched the second hand progress around the circle of numbers. For nine long months, I had marked the passage of time — checking off days, weeks, trimesters, and seasons on my calendar. When the doctor had finally held up the blood-streaked bundle of folded arms and

7

legs and declared my son perfect, I felt unutterably relieved. My baby might have reminded me of the bag of innards you pull out of a raw chicken, but he was okay! Not only okay, he was *perfect*. And his eyes — little azure almonds — were open! The breathless waiting and worrying was over.

But now I wanted to smash that noisy clock. The counting, it dawned on me, would never stop. I would count the time between feedings and wet diapers, the hours of sleep I wasn't getting, steps taken, words spoken, teeth lost, and finally the days until my child left home. A mother, I realized, counted until she died.

"Dr. Romph will be here as soon as she can make it," the pediatrician said, reappearing in my room the way rabbits do from magicians' hats. He peered at Malcolm in his isolette. "I was lucky to reach her."

He glanced at me and then away, as though wondering if he should say something more.

"The color on this baby is definitely off," he said, and crossed his arms at the chest, reminding me of Mr. Clean. I shrugged, not knowing what he was talking about.

"Usually," he added, "when I tell mothers their babies have heart murmurs, they cry." He fixed his eyes on a spot of wall above my head.

Dry-eyed, I stared at his face. Having always been one to expect bad news, the worst news, I now refused to believe I was hearing it. This couldn't be happening; there must be some mistake.

"It's most unusual for a new mother not to cry," he went on, still focusing on the blank space beyond me.

Was this his idea of a bedside manner? How dare he say something was wrong with my baby and then top it

8

off by implying I was somehow an inadequate mother for not crying in front of him. Was it supermomish of me *not* to weep? I wanted to scream at him to go away and never come back, but being at heart an obliging (or at least suggestible) patient, I felt tears spring to my eyes.

"That's better," the doctor said, as though he were talking to a little girl who had finally stopped poking at her peas and taken a bite. The doctor lingered for a moment and then disappeared. Once he was gone, my tears came in a flood.

Since Malcolm's birth, my body had sprung leaks everywhere. First the mucous plug had plopped out, followed by a rush of amniotic fluid and loose bowels. Then came a sudden full-bodied sweat, the kind that breaks out all over you in the sauna. Next, my breasts had dribbled a yellowish, premilk liquid. Now, my lip was bleeding, and my nose and eyes were flowing. Even during labor, when they had given me petocin to speed me up and each contraction had been an escalating bolt of searing pain, I hadn't lost control like this. Other women on the ward had bellowed and moaned, but I had been stoical. Now I felt murderously hormonal, like a vengeful goddess from Greek mythology.

There was something familiar about this scene. Had it happened before, in a dream? Hadn't I been dreading this moment all my life? I had always known it would come, always felt that a major catastrophe was stalking me, waiting to erupt. Was that why I feared doctors so much? Eventually, one of them was going to wallop me with a fateful blow. And this guy just had.

Someone else popped in the door. It was Bill, dressed in paint-speckled work pants and a torn T-shirt. He sat down on the bed and draped his slim arms around me, the pull of his body yanking at my fresh abdominal wound. He reeked of turpentine.

"Sorry I didn't clean myself up properly," he said. "I was painting the kitchen. But I wanted to get right over here."

My breaths came in hard, ragged stabs.

"I just saw the doctor in the hall," he said, his voice as comforting as a cup of hot tea with honey. "Everything's going to be fine."

There it was, my husband's eternal calm and optimism, two qualities I lacked the genes for.

Bill reached over and picked up Malcolm. A thin layer of sweat had appeared above his tiny lips. His breathing seemed faster and more labored. His baby cheeks, brushed with pink at birth, had faded to the color of skim milk.

We sat like stones, waiting. I stared at the clock, hoping the doctor would arrive before Bill had to leave to meet his mother's train. She was on her way up from New York City to see her new grandson.

"If the doctor comes while I'm gone, try to find out exactly what's wrong," Bill said. "Write it down."

We both knew I was the worst person for this task. Even when I went in fortified with a list of questions and asked every one of them, I would promptly forget the doctor's replies. To combat my selective memory lapses, I had begun recreating the conversations in my journal, which worked well enough on my monthly visits to the OB-GYN, the only time in my life I'd seen a doctor for anything more serious than poison ivy.

Bill wiped my face with a damp washcloth, smoothed back my hair for me, and left for the train station. Waiting,

I listened to the shrieking clock. The walls and window began to vibrate, like a Van Gogh painting. I could barely breathe. The nurses were whispering out in the hall, but no one came in. So much for the jocundity of the past days. Now they were avoiding me. Who would dare make jokes anymore about Malcolm's being "a lazy little man at the breast?" He wasn't lazy, he was sick! And they hadn't even noticed.

The ringing phone startled me. For days people had been calling to congratulate us on Malcolm's birth. We had told everyone we were disappointed about the cesarean, "But hey, we had a healthy baby boy!" What would I say now? I glared at the phone, willing it to stop. Finally it stopped, then started again. I picked up the receiver. It was Bill, calling to tell me his mother's train would be an hour late. I would have to face the cardiologist alone.

Fear swirled through my guts, like the wet colors in a child's finger painting. What exactly was a cardiologist, anyway? I had always made a point of knowing as little as possible about medicine and doctors, figuring that what I didn't know wouldn't hurt me. I couldn't comprehend those girls from high school who had volunteered as candy stripers in the hospital, delivering mail and reading magazines to sick people. The idea spooked me. Until I signed in to deliver Malcolm, I had not spent a night in a hospital. Nor had I been exposed to illness in others, my parents having carefully shielded me from the health problems of friends and family members.

Growing up, I had been the child with the runaway imagination, the emotional kid. Certain adults told me I exaggerated everything, made mountains out of molehills, like Dorothy in the *Wizard of Oz*.

"You're always getting yourself into a fret over nothing," Auntie Em told her. "Why don't you go find yourself a place where there isn't any trouble!"

I knew exactly how Dorothy felt.

Now, as I looked down at Malcolm, I thought I could see my son shriveling before my eyes. I didn't care who called me a Cassandra. Malcolm was turning into a wizened old man, on his way to death.

And I was terrified of him.

Dog Woman

Patty Romph looked at me and smiled. Her eyes reminded me of a Labrador retriever's — sad, with puffy, down-turning brows. As she came toward me, I could smell the out-of-doors on her, a loamy and slightly salty odor. I realized that, for the first time in my life, I hadn't breathed any fresh air for three whole days.

She held out a large, red, chapped hand, one that had obviously worked a spade, hauled rocks, and pulled weeds. "Sorry it took me so long to get here. I came as fast as I could."

She was a tall, almost gawky woman, with long, wavy brown hair flecked with gray; some of it had been pulled back, sloppily, into a barrette. She wore no make up. I guessed she was in her mid-forties. Under her buttoned lab coat, I could see corduroy pants, and she was wearing muddy, lace-up leather boots with rubber bottoms, like the kind advertised in the L. L. Bean catalog.

"One of my dogs got caught in a trap this morning," she explained. That was why she was muddy — and late.

"May I?" she asked, reaching for Malcolm. She gathered him into her arms, as though he were rare Chinese porcelain, and laid him carefully in his isolette. She swept her hair back and hunched over him, her stethoscope searching his tiny chest for clues.

There had been absolutely no reason to suspect anything would be wrong with my baby. At twenty-nine, I was robust, with sinewy muscles. I had recently quit dancing, but my ten-year career as a modern dancer had kept my body trim and flexible. Always a tomboy, I still relished an impromptu game of touch football and a good climbing tree. People said my stride was like my father's, and he had been a track star in college. I had inherited my dad's iron constitution. He never got sick, and neither did I. I had the boundless energy of an adolescent dog. Bill was healthy too. He suffered from occasional headaches, but they were never so severe that a few crushed aspirin in water wouldn't cure them.

Dr. Romph turned Malcolm onto his stomach and listened to his back. She shook her head slightly and held back a moment before she spoke. "I'm afraid Malcolm's a very sick baby," she said finally, straightening up and slipping her stethoscope into her lab-coat pocket. She picked him up and held him in her arms. "I can't tell from listening what's wrong with his heart, but it's definitely not pumping efficiently." She looked down at him with a tender, almost forlorn expression. "We need to get him on some medications right away and try to stabilize him, see how he responds. And we'll have to transfer him to a bigger hospital. Today."

I couldn't speak.

She handed Malcolm back to me and sat down in a chair next to my bed. How different she was from the last doctor, from any doctor I had ever encountered.

"I know this is very hard for you," she said. "And I'm so sorry."

I felt the corners of my mouth pull down, and a lump, like a pressing thumb, in my throat. But no tears came.

She asked if there was heart disease in my family or Bill's. Normally, I wouldn't even consider illness and my family in the same breath. We were healthy people. On my side, they seemed almost to *disapprove* of illness, scorning infirmities as though they were moral weaknesses or signs of a lack of will. Being ill was like being fat or lazy, a condition one should be able to control. Illnesses happened to other people in other families — not to industrious, sturdy types like us.

I shook my head.

"Do you remember being sick any time during your pregnancy?"

"No." I said. "Wait. I think I had some kind of flu early on."

"Really? How early?"

"I'm not sure right now." My head was throbbing and I felt panicky.

Dr. Romph pressed my arm gently. She told me she had to make a few phone calls, but that she'd be right back. "Will you be all right while I'm gone?"

I nodded. Before leaving the room, she gently pushed the box of tissues on my tray table closer to me.

"Try not to think about it," my mother had always advised me, whenever something unpleasant threatened to

14

happen or, God forbid, did happen. We were the proto-
typical American family of the 1950s: We didn't discuss
scary and painful feelings in our household. Denial was
our modus operandi.

And I did try hard not to think about bad things. But
any scary TV movie, glimpsed surreptitiously at my friend
Tracey's house, could disturb my sleep patterns for months
with horrific dreams that haunted my waking hours. No
one suspected my torment because I had learned to keep
it to myself. Unspoken, my fears thrived.

Being a dancer and an athlete, I knew and trusted my
body, on the outside. But I worried constantly about its
hidden, intracellular workings and about the possibility
of illness or grief or death bursting into my life. Now, all
my dread fulfilled, how was I supposed to think about
anything other than the fact that my beautiful pale son,
lying there in my arms, was critically ill?

I put Malcolm down on the bed beside me and reached
for my journal. Although "journal" hadn't been on the
Lamaze teacher's list of items to take to the hospital (along
with toothbrush, nightie, etc.), I had brought mine with
me. I took it almost everywhere, even sometimes to movies
so I could scribble down the good dialogue. Early on, I
had learned that just to record a slice of my life — a snatch
of overheard conversation, a fear, a dream — created a
helpful distance between me and my immediate experience. Once an image had been written down, it didn't
wield quite so much power over me.

I turned to the first blank page of my journal and wrote,

"I'm afraid Malcolm's a very sick baby," Dr. Romph said.

I stared at the page. Before writing more, I realized I would have to locate an earlier entry.

Thumbing through the dog-eared pages, I found what I was looking for. It was a conversation with my first OB-GYN, Dr. Harper, in New York, hastily scrawled while I was supposed to be getting dressed after the exam:

> *"One last thing!" He's leaving the room. It is now or never.*
> *"Yes?"*
> *"I was sick in the first few weeks."*
> *"Morning sickness?"*
> *"No. I think I had the flu or something."*
> *"Your symptoms?"*
> *"I was achy and had chills and bad swollen glands."*
> *"Any fever?"*
> *"Yeah."*
> *"How high?"*
> *"It got up there. Once it was 103."*
> *"Did you take anything?"*
> *"No, but I soaked in tepid baths."*
> *"Don't worry," he says. "Lots of women catch colds during pregnancy and deliver healthy babies. You're healthy and strong. I'm sure you'll do just fine." And then he's gone. . . .*
>
> *I'm giddy with relief and proud of myself for telling him about the high fever. For once, I didn't downplay my concern, make light of a situation I secretly took most seriously. The trouble is, I'm afraid of facts. If they aren't delivered in just the right way, I can put my own twisted spin on them, skew them to ignite my paranoia.*

The buzzing clock roared in my ears. I wondered what Dr. Romph was saying now to the people at Rhode Island Hospital. I didn't want to think about it. I turned back several pages and read more journal entries:

Dream: In my seventh month, I give birth prematurely to a golden retriever or maybe it's an Irish setter. The dog, named Dawn, is amazingly smart. When she's one day old, she already knows commands, like sit, lie down, roll over. She's big, almost full-grown, in only a few weeks. I feel guilty for wishing she were a baby and not a dog.

Do other pregnant women have such idiotic dreams?

Dream: Twelve little boys have been sliced down the middle of their chests. A man arrives who can mend the dead infants. We are struggling against a horrific queen who rules the land, but she is taking her daily swim in the dark lake now so we must make sure the man works fast to cure the little boys, before she returns.

Was it possible these dreams had been trying to tell me something was wrong with my child? Dr. Romph came back into the room. I closed my journal, slid it under the covers, and picked Malcolm up again. He felt like a damp rag doll, except that he was breathing very quickly.

I told her about the flu and my talk with Dr. Harper. She told me she too thought warm baths were curative. I marveled at this — a doctor saying she believed in something as folksy as soaking in lukewarm water. My mother, who swore by the healing powers of witch hazel, Epsom salts, vitamin C, and spirits of ammonia, would love this woman.

Dr. Romph asked me where I lived and somehow our new puppy, Molly, came up in the conversation. She seemed interested in everything about my dog, even wanting to know the colors of the other pups in the litter and how we had housebroken Molly.

"I have Samoyeds," she said. "And they keep me busy."

She had a soft, almost muted voice. Maybe it was her hushed quality that made me think she had a melancholic streak. I sensed that she didn't have children, that her dogs were her children. I wondered if she was married, but didn't ask.

Bill walked in with his mother, straight from the railroad station. They both looked pale and slit-lipped.

As Dr. Romph introduced herself, Bill's shoulders relaxed a notch and his jaw bones loosened their clamp on his teeth. I could see her quiet manner reassured him. She stood back while Bill's mom, Nancy, admired Malcolm.

"He looks just like Bill did as a baby," she said, her voice tentative. I could tell my mother-in-law was shocked. Clearly, this wasn't the joyous meeting she had so eagerly anticipated.

Malcolm would need to ride in an ambulance to Rhode Island Hospital. They would start him on an IV and medicines before he left. At the hospital there were places where we could sleep. Patty Romph removed my cesarean stitches, so we wouldn't have to think about them later, and arranged to have me discharged immediately.

How could I have complained, earlier in the morning, about the dismal hospital bed? Now I wanted nothing more than to stay in it, with my baby in my arms.

Keeping Vigil

I couldn't believe how far away my son was. The distance between Malcolm and me felt boundless, like a continent. Days earlier, we had been connected by living tissue; now thirty miles of black asphalt separated us. As Bill, Nancy, and I drove past row houses, factories, and green exit signs,

I was appalled by the fact that Malcolm had already made this trip *by himself*. New babies weren't supposed to go places, miles away, without their mothers.

The hospital loomed before us, an imposing nineteenth-century brick structure with turrets and towers that reminded me of a Victorian orphanage. Staring up at our destination, this huge ugly building, I couldn't fathom the harsh fact that my son, fresh from the warm waters of my womb, was somewhere inside it.

The first glimpse of Malcolm sent my heart rushing up into my throat and made my swollen breasts ache. He was one of several naked infants, all lying on their backs in a row, on what I would later learn were called "light tables." These were waist-high steel platforms on wheels, each with its bank of suspended lights that shone down on the bare-bottomed babies, warming them like slabs of roast beef in a cafeteria line. Malcolm's body was propped up at an angle, his head higher than his feet. His arms and legs were restrained by cuffs of gauze pinned to the white sheet beneath him. He lay spread-eagle, as though poised to make a snow angel. There was an IV line taped to his inner wrist and a monitor of some sort attached to his chest. A rectangle of blond hair had been shaved from the side of his head and the area pierced by another needle. A plastic tube protruded from his penis.

Malcolm's eyes were open, his head turned to the side. He seemed to be intently observing the other babies down the line, all of them screaming. Over all their heads, jagged lines rushed across small green screens, peaking and falling like measurements on a seismograph. Numbers flashed. Machines gurgled and beeped.

Behind me, a square-jawed doctor, with a clipboard under his arm, was talking to Bill and Nancy. He told them the staff was trying to stabilize Malcolm with "meds," so they could perform an angiography to find out what exactly was wrong.

I was relieved Nancy had insisted on coming with us to the hospital. Unlike me, she was tough and pragmatic, a strong presence. Doctors didn't scare her.

"When he's strong enough," the doctor said, "we'll shoot dye into his bloodstream, through an incision in the groin, and thread wires up into his heart." The dye would illuminate the pumping action of the heart and help show trouble spots. It was dangerous, but necessary for an accurate diagnosis.

"Right now," he added, "the baby is too sick for the procedure."

I stopped listening. All I wanted was to unshackle my son, swaddle him in my arms, and escape from that glaring inferno.

Some babies, the doctors told us, are born with three, occasionally two, and sometimes only one of the four chambers necessary for a complete, viable heart. A missing chamber is a devastating diagnosis. The heart can also be torn, like weak fabric, and need stitching. Often these tears, or holes, in the heart close on their own. Where they are located can determine how seriously they affect the pumping of the heart and what kind of intervention is called for. Valves, the cup-shaped stoppers that facilitate blood flow by opening and closing, can be stiff and function poorly, causing blood to pool behind them. Or they can be missing altogether, a most serious defect. These were only a few of the possible scenarios the doctors mentioned.

No one was willing to speculate any further, at least with us, about Malcolm's diagnosis and prognosis. All we could do was hope his condition would stabilize and that he wouldn't die before the angiography (referred to among hospital insiders as the "cath," short for catheterization). We had to hope the procedure itself wouldn't kill him, which was another possibility.

What had been touted as sleeping quarters for parents turned out to be one smoke-filled lounge furnished with Naugahyde recliners, a few short love seats, and a blaring television. (Why did every waiting room in America have to contain a huge, yammering TV?) In the main corridor outside, a heavy metallic door slammed shut after anyone ventured through it. This noise was guaranteed to wake up any parent lucky enough to be catching a few winks on a recliner or scrunched up on a love seat. No wonder the room was empty.

The hours inched by and became days. Bill came and went. He took several trips home to take care of Molly and the house and dropped his mother at the train station when she had to return to New York. But I didn't leave the hospital for days, convinced my son would fail — or vanish — if I took my eyes off him for too long.

Most of the time I sat and sweated in a rocking chair at Malcolm's side, my jaws and neck feeling as if they were being squeezed in an ever-tightening vice. Occasionally I took brief breaks to pump my throbbing breasts in the ladies room. I knew I wanted to breastfeed my son and, even though I couldn't feed him my milk then, I'd have to keep my breasts producing if I wanted to be able to nurse him later. It pained me to flush the milk down the toilet, but in those first days I didn't know what else to do with it.

One evening when I returned to the light table from a pumping break, Bill was crouching by Malcolm's side, his head of graying brown curls next to Malcolm's, his eyes following Malcolm's gaze.

"I wonder what he's staring at?" Bill had said. "All I see from this angle is the tile drop-ceiling." But Malcolm seemed to see something more; his eyes were big and round and full, like illuminated blue globes. Was he seeing an angel? Death? God? I stroked his head, hoping the motion would make him close his eyes or blink, but he continued to stare.

The night nurse, Kathy, approached us. She was young and small-waisted, with a frizzy blond perm and a perfectly made-up face. Everything about her was pristine, such a contrast to me. My shirt was stained with milk, my dirty blond hair tangled and sweaty, my blue eyes pink and puffy.

"This might comfort him," she said, taping a red bottle-top nipple to a washcloth and handing it to me. I put the nipple to Malcolm's lips and he sucked furiously, his eyes rolling back into his head with pleasure.

"I've never seen such a patient baby," Kathy said. "He's using all his energy to get better, not to fuss."

I tried to smile, but moving my face muscles made my cheeks hurt. They were chapped, the way lips get when the weather's about to change. My right eye wouldn't stop twitching. I knew she could see the terror in my face.

"Is he going to die?" I asked, in a sudden reflex, and immediately regretted my words. How could she know? And being asked would only make her night shift even tougher than it already was.

"I'm afraid I can't answer that," she said gently.

"I know you can't. I'm sorry."

Bill put his arm around my shoulder and eased me into my chair. Kathy told me there was an in-hospital chapel I could visit, but I declined the offer. I hadn't been in a church since my wedding, almost seven years earlier. It had been ages since I'd rejected my father's dour Quakerism and my mother's Episcopal leanings. But I had always considered myself to be a spiritual, if not a religious, person.

Incredibly, I had never attended a funeral or seen a body laid out in a coffin. My only up-close brush with death had been the occasional goldfish found floating belly-up in the fish tank, and I would sob over it before spooning a shallow grave in the backyard. When my grandmother died, I was away at college. Not wanting to upset me, my parents didn't tell me about her until weeks later, long after the funeral. I was also away at college when my childhood dog died. Again, my parents held back the truth until I arrived home for Thanksgiving. By then, all traces of the beloved mutt had vanished — her bowl, leash, collar, and dog towels. She had disappeared without a trace, never to be dwelled on again. This seemed to be the WASP way of coping with tragedy.

I rocked gently in my chair, wishing now that I had the habit of prayer, like the woman several light tables down. She had hovered over her daughter all one afternoon, her head bowed and eyes closed, her hands clasped in front of her nose, her face serene. Returning from one of my trips to the ladies room, I noticed that both the infant girl and her mother were gone, the light table starkly bare. Had a miraculous healing occurred . . . or a death? I couldn't bring myself to ask.

Finally, after a week, the doctors decided Malcolm's heart failure was no longer too acute for the cath. Now, at last, the doctors would figure it all out; the suspense would be over. Not knowing any better, Bill and I were falling into the simplistic thinking common to hospital neophytes: that medical diagnoses were precise, like sharply focused black-and-white pictures, and solutions existed for all problems. Of course the doctors could fix whatever was wrong. Did our son have an operable condition? Would he survive a surgical procedure? These questions would be answered decisively.

Bill and I waited anxiously in the parents' lounge. We held hands and sat on a plaid love seat, startling each time the metal door at the end of the corridor slammed shut. We listened to the clamor of the orderlies rolling trays of rattling supplies down the hall. The hospital support people, the underlings, always seemed happy, calling out to each other with remarks like, "Hey Man! What's shakin'?" and cracking jokes in the hallways. Apparently they were immune to the despair around them.

I scribbled in my journal:

Sitting here with Bill, I wonder if there could be any mutual purgatory worse than waiting for news of our child's fate. Bill slumps deeper into the couch, his hands clasped between his knobby knees. His skin is drawn drum-taut across his smooth, pale face; all signs of a healthy end-of-summer glow have vanished. His cheek bones jut out more sharply than usual. He still has blue kitchen paint on his neck and ear. THIS PROCEDURE IS TAKING HOURS LONGER THAN THEY SAID IT WOULD.

When Dr. Romph walked in, Bill and I jumped up expectantly.

She was smiling. "Malcolm really impressed everybody," she said. Most babies scream at the beginning of the procedure, but he had been calm and amenable. The little guy was too smart to waste any energy complaining.

"He had all four heart chambers," she said, which was great news. He did have an ASD (atrium septal defect), or hole in his heart wall, but it was operable. It was his valves they weren't so sure about, especially the mitral valve. That was the one, she explained, through which blood pumped out of the heart into the body. The cath pictures weren't detailed enough to show the precise workings of the valves. But, if they were deficient, there was always the possibility of replacing them with prosthetic valves — from pigs. And she was going to make sure her associate, Dr. Casteneda at Boston Children's Hospital, would be the one to operate on Malcolm. Casteneda, she informed us, was the best pediatric cardiac surgeon in the world.

We listened like good students, clueless to the dangers and the unpredictability of heart surgery or the unreliability of prosthetics. All we heard was that Malcolm was going to live; his condition was "operable." That word echoed in our ears, instantly becoming our mantra.

Our task now was to strengthen him, Dr. Romph told us, to get him to grow before surgery.

"Bigger babies fare better, as do older, larger hearts," she said. "Sometimes infants start improving for no apparent reason and if that happens we could gain even more time before surgery. We'll have to wait and see."

I had never been good at waiting and seeing. I needed my life's issues to be solved instantly.

Wakefield

Everyone was telling me I should go home for a night and get some rest.

Home. "Where was home?" I wondered, my mind dumb from stress and sleeplessness. Home certainly wasn't the house in Wakefield, Rhode Island. From the day we had moved in, four months back, the place had been in a perpetual state of renovation, the rooms torn up and full of plaster dust. Our tiny, two-room Greenwich Village apartment, which we'd had to give up because I was pregnant and it was too small, seemed more like home.

We had chosen Wakefield because we knew the area; some friends of my parents had a summer house there and we had visited them. The town was on the Amtrak line between Boston and New York. Bill, a freelance writer, had corporate clients in both cities. And I could do my current job, marketing audiovisual shows, from anywhere around New York.

Before buying a house, sensible people research the market, walk the neighborhoods, assess the schools, compare taxes. Not us. Having moved many times in our married life—from Boston to New York to Los Angeles to Maine and back to New York—we were used to tossing our stuff into duffel bags and heading west or east, north or south, knowing we'd eventually find digs once we got where we were going.

We had driven around Wakefield and I already knew the area where we would intensify our search. My mother, a real estate broker, had taught me the oldest cliché in her business: location, location, location. Like her, I could always find the "right" neighborhood, at least the economy version.

But we'd had no time to waste. The baby was due in September and it was already April. We put in a bid on a house at the end of our first day of looking. Who cared that the kitchen had only a broken refrigerator and an old stove, no counters, no sink? On the bright side, our monthly expenses would barely go up, yet we would have an eight-room house in an old, established neighborhood.

At the end of May, we moved, vowing to have the house fixed up before the baby's due date, September 16. Bill and I definitely weren't "handyman types"—Bill liked to say the only tool in his tool box was a phone—but we got to work, steaming wallpaper off walls, scraping linoleum off the maple floors, and painting. We hired a contractor who changed entrances, sealed off doors and built closets. My family visited and pitched in. We got our dog Molly.

Outside, I rototilled a sunny area of lawn and put in a vegetable garden, much to the dismay of the elderly woman next door, who shook her head in disapproval at the "man's work" I was doing, and in my condition.

All summer, we kept a watchful eye on the calendar as we moved from room to room, trying to sleep in the least disrupted spot in the house. Finally, we had the kitchen in working order, a new entrance foyer, the floors all over the house polyurethaned, closets built in the master bedroom, and, most important, the baby's room ready — all before Malcolm was born.

Go home and rest, Dr. Romph was telling me now. But, without Malcolm, I didn't want to go back to that house. We had moved in and fixed the place up for *him*. For him, I would gladly brave sleepless nights curled up in the rocker or endlessly pace the floor in the hospital lounge. Even in the Rhode Island Hospital sleeping area, which was more like the Port Authority bus terminal, staying was infinitely preferable to being forty-five minutes away in a house that seemed almost to mock us for daring to think we could plan our future.

"Go home," Bill and Dr. Romph insisted, "just for one night."

"But my parents are coming up from Princeton to help out," I said. "I'll go home when they get here. They'll make the place more cheerful."

"You've got to go now," Dr. Romph said. "You need sleep to stay healthy. And if you don't stay healthy, how are you going to be able to care for your baby?"

That did it. I went home. But I couldn't sleep. Instead I spent anxious hours roaming through the rooms of our house, worrying about what was happening to Malcolm in my absence, and calling the night nurse at regular intervals for updates on his condition: "Is his IV spot red?" "Did he keep the meds down?" I always saved the hardest question for last: "Has he been crying?"

I lay on the living room couch, hugging Molly and

waiting until morning. Eons ago it seemed, in the throes of labor, I had parked my bloated body on this same couch. Looking back on my pregnant self, I realized now what a state of innocence I had enjoyed. I had known nothing about hospitals, intensive care units, broken hearts. Or about how one fateful listen with a stethoscope could thrust a family into a living hell.

Now I knew the daunting truth: The human condition was unbearably precarious. My life was completely out of my control. Knowing what I now knew, I couldn't imagine ever again living a normal existence, whatever that was.

Fish Bowl Life

As always when I returned to the Pediatric Intensive Care (PIC), I performed the required entry ritual. I scrubbed my hands and forearms with a powerful antibacterial soap, slipped a sterile hospital robe on over my clothes, removed my shoes, and slid my feet into sterile paper slippers. It was a laborious procedure, but I was amazed at how quickly it had become routine, and almost comforting.

Every day, it seemed, new medical glitches appeared: rashes, erratic respirations, a high bilirubin count, monitors malfunctioning, medicines vomited up, other babies in acute distress. Hospital life was so frustrating because no one seemed to know why anything happened. Reasons were always speculative: This *might* be causing that, "But we aren't sure." And misinformation, we were learning, rampaged through a hospital like a virus, with no one ever knowing where it came from. Was there really an outbreak of meningitis on the unit? Who knew?

"Hey, Malcolm's mom!"

Looking around, I saw a short, stout woman with dark closely cropped hair. She was wearing a Mickey Mouse T-shirt. I had seen her before, but she had always been surrounded by a passel of young children, her own I assumed, so we hadn't spoken to each other. I waved at her.

"I'm Andrew's mom," she said, pointing to the crib by her side. "I've been around this place a long time. If you need anything, just ask me."

"Thanks." I didn't feel like talking.

"Mind if I join you?" she asked, scraping a hard plastic chair across the floor in her wake.

"No, that's fine." A cloud of despair mushroomed inside my chest.

"Even when it's bad," she pointed at Malcolm, who was lying under special bilirubin lights, with black patches over his eyes, "it's worse when you're not here, isn't it?"

"Yeah," I said.

She told me she missed Andrew when she was home, but she and her husband had five other children. She had to be with them sometimes. "You got other kids?"

"No," I said. There was no other way to say it. Suddenly I wished she would go away.

"That lounge is an insult," she said, undaunted by my silence. "But when it's not crowded in here, I've slept on a cot by Andrew's crib. Sometimes you can find one around the hospital. It's like hitting pay dirt when you do."

She told me about Andrew. He was two and had undergone three surgeries. He was scheduled for one more operation — the final one, they hoped. The more I was learning, the more scared I was becoming. There seemed to be no end to these wretched cardiac scenarios. Hospitals weren't only full of sick people, I was finding out, they were also full of other people's pain and stories. It was impossible to be immune to the suffering of those around you. The PIC was one large room, a glass cage. Everyone's life traumas were in full view. Their horror became intermingled with your horror.

Andrew's mom asked me about Malcolm. I told her he would eventually have surgery at Boston Children's Hospital.

"You just wouldn't believe the doctors there," she said. "They work miracles every day. All Andrew's surgeries have been at Children's."

"Oh," I said, unable to muster any enthusiasm for surgery on babies.

"This place is totally primitive compared to Boston," she said. "But here's a tip that makes me feel better. If you want to know what goes on when you're not here, peek at his chart when the nurses are out of the room. Everything's in there."

A nurse entered the unit and walked over to Andrew's space.

"You looking for us?" Andrew's mother said.

"They're ready for his tests downstairs," the nurse said.

"Well, they can just wait until he wakes up," she said. "I had him up and ready when they told me, and then nobody came. So they can just wait."

The nurse shrugged and headed toward the door.

"I better talk to her," Andrew's mom said. Halfway across the room she stopped, turned to me, and nodded her head once in a precisely affirmative gesture that said: "It's the parents who rule around here." I nodded back.

Before she left that night, Andrew's mom found me a cot.

Out of the corner of my eye, I glanced at the new baby and her mother. They had just arrived that morning. The woman clutched the side of her daughter's isolette. Her hands were white and veiny. The daughter, who had a beautiful heart-shaped face, had been born with her stomach on the outside; it was exposed and looked like a piece of uncooked liver. One of her thin legs dangled uselessly at an odd angle to her body. I had overheard a doctor say she was missing the femur bone and had a hole in her pelvis.

The mother told the day nurse, Elaine, that her husband wouldn't be able to come see the baby often. He was a fisherman and had to go to work every morning before dawn. She wanted to be here but was afraid to drive into the city alone.

Listening in on other people's private talk had always been one of my bad habits. Sometimes when Bill and I were out for dinner, he would see a familiar distant look in my eyes and whisper, "Okay, so what's happening at the table behind you." Now, I could do without the habit. What I overheard and witnessed around here, I didn't want to know: The fisherman's wife screaming and doubling over with abdominal pain (or was it grief?); the arrogant, patriarchal cardiologist who ignored his patients' parents during rounds and spoke only to his residents in scary medical jargon; the orphaned baby who screamed twenty-four hours a day.

Whenever something upsetting happened to anybody in the ICU, I wrote the scene down in my journal. I didn't know what else to do. Andrew's mom scurried around, trying to help everybody, which amazed me because, at that time in my life, I didn't easily give comfort.

Since Malcolm's birth, I had barely noticed anything outside the hospital. The outdoors, where I had always felt most at home, had become lost to me. In the natural world, I now felt like an alien, so used was I to unnatural lighting, regulated temperatures, plastic, steel, linoleum — the sterile hospital world.

But I knew I had to be there. From the start, Dr. Romph had encouraged Bill and me to stay closely involved with Malcolm's care. All too often, she told us, parents just assume they're powerless and let everybody else run the show. I read and reread her advice, recorded in my journal:

"Inform yourselves about every aspect of Malcolm's care. Don't be afraid to ask questions of doctors and nurses. Find out what the meds are called and why they're being given, how often they're being given and what the exact doses are.

"You're the ones who know your child best. Don't let anyone try to tell you differently. You two are the consistent elements in his life. Nurses and doctors change shifts. Parents are constants. Don't ever hesitate to speak up on Malcolm's behalf. You have to be his advocates."

In the two weeks since Malcolm's birth, I — who, as a little girl, never played "Mother" the way my girlfriends did — was now consumed with a fierce maternal passion for my baby.

Plans

It was a stunning fall day and Bill had convinced me to take a short walk around the Brown University campus. We had browsed in a bookstore and then, at an outdoor cafe, ordered a dark beer (allegedly good for lactation).

As we sat in the slanty, late afternoon sun, Bill started talking about the future. Looking at him, I noticed that his curls, in recent weeks, had gone grayer.

"Every day is so overwhelming, I know," he said, his Roman nose wrinkling against the glare. "But we need to make some plans."

"Plans?" I asked. I could barely plan when to go to the bathroom these days.

Bill looked away and lowered his head. I knew he felt guilty. His work schedule made it so that he could only come and go sporadically. He wasn't free to be at the hospital around the clock, as I was. I had taken an indefinite unpaid leave from my job. He couldn't.

I noticed his face looked remarkably like Malcolm's, except that now Bill had deep creases under his eyes. He was exhausted, not only from the demands of work — his meetings with clients, the daily driving he was doing from Boston to Wakefield to the hospital, the ordeal with Malcolm — but also from bearing the responsibility for updating friends and relatives on Malcolm's condition.

The word was out. People called day and night. The most recent cards and letters expressed alarm and offers of help. When Bill was home, he spent hours on the phone. Over and over again, he explained Malcolm's condition and, despite his own anguish, tried to console everybody else. At the hospital, he brought me lists of the people who had called and what they had said. I didn't want to talk to anybody; their sympathy made me feel like crying, and I was doing enough of that already, in the hospital's bathroom stalls.

Bill had been thinking about a lot of things.

"I think we should move back to Boston and soon," he said. "Most of my clients are there, and commuting from Wakefield is absurd. Plus, it's clear that Malcolm is going to need to live near Boston Children's Hospital."

"But we've done so much to fix the house up," I said. "What's everybody going to think if we move so soon?"

"You know what?" Bill said, taking a swallow of beer. "I don't give a damn what anybody thinks. Boston is where we belong. A house is just a house. They're everywhere. We can get another one."

"What about my job in New York?" I said. "I can't do the work from Boston."

"That's true," Bill said. "So quit. I'll hire you. You can write scripts for me. You already have. I'll help you get your own clients."

Bill was completely unconventional and I had always appreciated that quality in him, even though his life dreams sometimes seemed, to my negative bent, absurdly impractical. If we decided to sell a house, six months after buying it, that was our business. Who said you had to stay in a house just because you'd fixed it up or keep a job just because you'd taken it?

"Remember," Bill said, quietly. "This is just a phase. Life is going to change after Malcolm has surgery. We'll be able to care for him at home, wherever home is, and we'll both be able to do other things too. I'm determined to finish my novel, and you know you want to get your own writing going."

I nodded, trying to feel hopeful. Bill was ten years older than I was and had a wider perspective on life. But he was straining too. I could hear the sadness, the tremor in his voice. He had been so excited about everything — starting a family, finishing his first novel, working out of New York and Boston. Now his voice was flat, hushed by reality. We sat in silence, feeling the warm sun on our faces.

To me, our words and plans sounded hollow, almost false, next to the enormity of Malcolm's life-and-death situation. We were talking a good game, but we both knew the future loomed before us, treacherous and unknown.

Back at the hospital, Dr. Romph was waiting for us.

"What's wrong?" I asked, feeling my legs go weak and instantly regretting the time we'd spent dawdling at a cafe.

"Nothing's wrong," she said. "I just wanted to talk with the two of you."

"What is it?" I asked.

She was looking at me in a way she never had before, as if she were sizing me up, somehow. Something *was* wrong.

"Well, I guess you haven't heard," she said. "I'm planning to send Malcolm home — tomorrow."

I was stunned. I had been vigorously promoting the idea with the nurses, getting them to teach me how to give his meds and keep the records, but I never thought we would go so soon. Only two days had passed since Malcolm had been unwired from the heart monitor. Holding him without being able to track his beats on the machine still made me uneasy.

Dr. Romph said there was too much diarrhea and too many colds up on the pediatric floor. Moving him there would be risky, even to a private room.

"You can handle him at home," she said and smiled. "You're with him all the time anyway, Carol. You may as well be somewhere comfortable."

I'll never forget her next words: "You need to have some fun with Malcolm," she said.

I inhaled sharply. Maybe what she was really saying was for me to try to enjoy my son while he lasted. I sensed she knew something else too: Malcolm might die at home and home was a far better place than the hospital to die.

Why, I wondered, did I always put a negative, hysterical twist on everything?

Home!

"How do you like it?" I asked Malcolm. He was cradled in my left arm. With my right, I made a sweeping gesture that took in the whole bedroom. Malcolm looked around with his characteristic wide-eyed interest, all the while sucking vigorously on his red pacifier. I laid him in his crib, wished for my camera, and swiped at the tears that were already overflowing my eyes.

"Get a grip," I told myself. "Be positive."

We looked at the Japanese maple tree outside his window. When a gust of wind rustled the brilliant maroon leaves, Malcolm stopped sucking and seemed to gape at the sight, awestruck. His pacifier fell to the floor. Over the summer I had spent hours surveying the yard, from a low branch of that red maple. I still loved the thrill of picking a good climber, grabbing a smooth, cool branch and hoisting myself up, limb by limb in a dizzying progress toward the splendor at the top. I hoped someday Malcolm would experience the joy of hiding in a canopy of leaves, high above the earthly concerns of toiling humans.

I looked down at my wan baby. He was studying my face as though he knew I was thinking bittersweet thoughts. I forced a smile and squeezed him gently. Now that it was just the two of us, I could no longer disappear down the corridor for a sudden cry, leaving the nurses in charge. Having signed on as doctor, nurse, and heart monitor, as well as mother, I was in charge of every shift. Babies, like puppies, could sense the vibes from the humans around them; I was convinced of this. For Malcolm's sake, I had to exude a spirit of hope and calm, no matter how desperate I felt deep down. It was a tall order for me. My mission: Get him strong for surgery.

The first night at home we all snuggled in our bed, Malcolm nestled between Bill and me. At last we were all spending the night under the same roof, sharing the same sheets!

Eventually, I dozed off. When I woke up an hour later, the sheets were soaked in my postpartum sweat and Malcolm was watching me with that steady, knowing gaze of his. I reached for him. He felt clammy and chilled but didn't seem the least bit bothered by his condition. I thought babies were supposed to cry when they were wet and cold. As I pulled him close to me, he continued to study my face. What was he thinking?

Bill loved to create schedules, systems, and work plans, not that we ever followed them for long, but the design and production phases made him feel efficient. Now he made charts to help us keep organized records of Malcolm's daily activities. On one sheet of paper, we would mark the time and then the activity: pee, poop, heart rate, respiration rate, grunting, sweating, sleeping, unusual behavior. On a separate sheet was the meds schedule with times of day already entered and the meds listed: Diuril, Lasix, digitalis. All we had to do was check off the box after we gave him the med. Later, Bill would squeeze in another two columns: "spit up med," "kept med down."

We had workmen coming to insulate the crawl spaces around the house. Holding Malcolm, I hauled furniture away from the upstairs walls with my free arm, to give the men access to their work area.

Bill and I had debated canceling all home improvements. But it had been hard to get a contractor lined up and we didn't want to have to do it all over again later. No matter what happened with Malcolm, we were now sure we wanted to sell the house, and showing a half-renovated home wouldn't be smart.

While the men banged hammers upstairs, I sat with Malcolm on my lap, in a square of sun that spread invitingly across the couch. Having strangers stomping around was disconcerting, but compared to the wide-open hospital, home seemed luxuriously private.

Malcolm seemed to be enjoying the relaxing heat. He had never felt warm rays of natural light on his face, only the artificial fluorescence of the hospital. I nursed him in the sun and, as was his habit, he held my little finger in his hand. What bliss! I sensed he was starting to breathe faster, but tried to ignore his quickened chest motion. We were going to relax at home; I was determined about that. Yet he did seem to be laboring for breath . . . or was I only imagining things? Reluctantly, I checked his heart rate. It was much too high, alarmingly high. I rushed into the kitchen, with Malcolm in my arms, and marked his chart. How stupid of me to have put him in the sun and to have let him nurse! The heat and effort had made his rate soar.

Now he was sweating and grunting. Right there in the kitchen I stripped him down to his diaper. It had been so much fun treating him for once like a regular baby, dressing him in a little outfit from his bureau drawer, even though I'd tried not to notice how his skinny body swam in even the smallest newborn size. But the cute little stretchy suit I had selected that morning had probably made him hotter.

I checked his diaper. It was dry. According to the schedule, he hadn't peed since 3:00 A.M., and he'd been feeding most of the night. Kidney failure. If he didn't urinate soon, I'd have to call Patty Romph. I wrote myself a note about this and fanned him with a magazine, hoping to cool him down.

I took him upstairs.

"We just need to get a clean outfit," I said to the workmen, certain they could hear the forced cheerfulness in my voice. I wished, more than anything, that they weren't there. As I walked around, I kept a smile plastered on my face, trying to pretend everything was fine, that I wasn't frantic about my baby's condition. I had been the same around the nurses and the doctors. Even when I felt unutterably miserable, I always tried to seem jovial and upbeat.

Frank, the man in charge, glanced at me and frowned. He pushed his red baseball cap up and wiped his brow. He looked worried. About me? No, most likely he wasn't even thinking about us; he was probably concentrating on that small space he was going to have to crawl into. Why the hell did I *care* so much what the workmen thought of me or my circumstances? What difference did it make? These guys were strangers I would never have to see again. So what if I looked upset?

I seemed to fear — and all my life had desperately tried to avoid — being the subject of people's sympathy. I would never have made a scene the way the fisherman's wife had. The workmen had looked at me and then quickly turned away, eyes down, like I was some lowly creature they pitied, a powerless victim of circumstance. There was no way around the bald facts. We had moved here to raise our baby and he was hovering at death's door. Ours was potentially a pitiful scenario and I felt exposed, weak, vulnerable. But I wasn't about to show my feelings.

I found Malcolm a lightweight sleeping suit, slammed the bureau drawers, and retreated again to the study off the kitchen.

A loud crash from upstairs made Malcolm flinch. I dressed him and then checked my watch. It was time for a feeding, to be followed by his dose of Lasix. I opted for the breast over bottled milk. It was much easier and more pleasant, even though I couldn't mark his exact intake on the chart afterward.

Malcolm ate well. For the moment, we were a new mother and baby at home, just like all the others. Life was good, great. I propped him up with pillows on the couch, knowing I needed two hands to prepare his meds. He looked like a little king on a throne! When I had everything ready, I gathered him into my lap and eased the blunt syringe into his mouth. He took the medicine down

41

easily. Terrific. I was beginning to feel like a pro. Waiting for the Lasix to settle, I was careful to hold him with his head higher than his body.

Suddenly, he threw up all over himself, me, and the couch. I could see the medicine in the milk. I cursed myself for not having burped him better after he ate. What about the meds? Should I give them again immediately or wait until the next feeding? I would have to ask Patty Romph about that too. And now I would have to go back upstairs for more baby clothes, with those men up there. I wanted the house to myself. Damn the home improvement.

Malcolm was breathing hard again. I recorded his respirations and heart rate; both were still too high. As I was walking through the house to go upstairs, the doorbell rang. I froze. Visitors weren't allowed; we were supposed to be living in a self-imposed quarantine. I looked at my watch — 1:00 P.M. There was something important about that hour. What was it?

Through the glass in the door, I saw an elderly woman with what looked like a small doctor's bag in one hand. The visiting nurse! Patty Romph had told me I had an appointment at 1:00 P.M. How could I have forgotten? I rushed to open the door and introduce myself.

"I understand there's a sick baby in the house," she said.

She looked at Malcolm in my arms. He was covered with yellowish white spit-up. The woman's thin lips turned up slightly at the corners. Was it a look of disgust?

"We're in the middle of renovations, so pardon the mess," I said. "Let's go to the back of the house where things are tidier."

Her eyes went straight to the spit-up on the couch. "I was just getting ready to clean this up," I said, trying to sound perky, like June Cleaver. "Why don't you sit in the chair and I'll get a change of clothes for Malcolm and tidy up a bit."

"As you wish," she said — an oddly formal phrase, I thought — and sat down, her knees pressing together.

The nurse listened to Malcolm's heart for a long time.

"I simply can't believe any doctor would let you bring such a sick baby home," she said, finally. She shook her head as if to say, "What'll those crazy doctors do next?"

"And you're so tired," she said, suddenly staring at me, her eyes dark and shiny, like a hawk's. "You're not up to this."

I told her I was feeling stressed at the moment. "Really, we're doing fine," I lied. How could she tell I'd only had about ten hours of sleep in the past two weeks?

"Well," she said, her tone softening. "You've got our number if you need it. I should check your incision while I'm here."

I showed her my scar.

"What are these?" she asked, pointing at a cluster of red bumps on my belly.

"Flea bites," I said. I told her my parents had come and taken our puppy, Molly, but she left fleas behind. We were going to flea-bomb the house but then suddenly Malcolm got to come home. So we'd have to wait to exterminate.

I didn't need to look at her to imagine her expression. I felt like Bill's Irish grandmother, who had said about herself, "I open my mouth and my brains fly out." My face was pink and I was shaking. How I longed to be one of those women with a sturdy, unflappable persona.

She left me her card and promised to be back the next day at the same time. When Patty Romph had told me a visiting nurse would come each day, I imagined a young friendly woman, similar to the nurses I had been surrounded by in recent weeks. We had talked and laughed and fussed over Malcolm together. The nurses were comrades, almost friends. They had made life bearable. But this woman? Yikes! She was steely, judgmental, humorless.

But maybe she was right. Maybe Malcolm *was* too sick to be at home. Maybe Dr. Patty Romph was a maverick. But the alternative? Returning to all those germs could kill him.

I knew I needed to talk to Patty Romph about his kidneys, but I hesitated. I wasn't sure I wanted to hear what she would say. That was one reason I resisted calling doctors. Another was that I always felt I was pestering them. "But that's part of their job," Bill would tell me. "To be bothered by you."

And at times there was something offhanded, almost laconic about Patty Romph. Was I imagining it? Sometimes she seemed distracted — unavailable, almost cold. I wondered if her distant manner had to do with our refusal to baptize Malcolm. She was a devout Catholic and had asked us a number of times to consider having him christened. Being agnostics, we found that ritual meaningless. There was no particular rush to baptize him anyway. He was going to live, wasn't he? We were trying to be positive and hopeful about that. Baptism had become synonymous, in our minds, with giving up on our son, with accepting defeat, with death.

The phone rang. It was Patty Romph. I told her everything.

I had read somewhere that delirious old men on their death beds often carried on conversations with former co-

44

workers. Women on the brink of death called out for their mothers. I knew one thing: This new mother, stranded at home with her sick baby, needed a mother herself.

I called mine in New Jersey and she agreed to come that night.

Not only did Mother immediately roll up her sleeves and tackle the piles of dirty laundry and dishes, she also shopped for food, bought witch hazel and cotton balls for our burning flea bites, cooked, and, most important, kept me company. She was the only person besides Bill who experienced, with me, the full brunt of living, hour by tortuous hour, with a critically ill infant. I was incredibly grateful to have a witness.

Every night I lie awake listening to Malcolm's breathing, terrified that if I sleep, his heart will stop and the grunting that petrifies me will cease. Mornings, I strip him down and lay him on the dreaded scale the visiting nurse lent me. The pointer always hovers at around 6 lb. 12 oz. Clearly, my son isn't beginning to thrive at home, the way Patty Romph said some babies do.

Because neither Bill nor I slept well when Malcolm was in our bed, Mother bought us a cot to put in his room. That way I'd be able to sleep beside his crib.

"Consider it an anniversary present," she said. Ours was in a few days, but Bill and I didn't have the energy to celebrate. We got a rueful laugh, however, at the idea of the wife getting her own roll-away bed as an anniversary gift.

She also suggested I stop weighing Malcolm every day; not only did being stripped and held against the cold, uncomfortable steel upset him — it was depressing for me. "We'll notice," she said, the wise mother of three healthy children, "if he starts gaining weight."

45

I read him The Cat in the Hat Comes Back, Harold and the Purple Crayon, and Goodnight Moon, some of my childhood favorites. I show him art books, explaining to him about nineteenth-century American landscape paintings and the twentieth-century regionalists. I put on Strauss and Sibelius and dance around the downstairs rooms, my son in my arms. By day and by night, Bill and I record everything on the charts. We make several trips to the emergency room at Rhode Island Hospital, wondering all the way if he would live until we got there. I never sleep for more than an hour or two. I'm afraid I might explode, I'm so full of love and fear.

One afternoon, after the nurse had finished examining Malcolm, Mother offered her a cup of tea, which she accepted, to my surprise — in our dump! The two of them chatted amiably, sitting together in their "sensible" shoes, wool skirts, and, I imagined, full slips underneath. I'll bet the nurse, like my mother, wore scratchy wool undershirts in the winter.

After two weeks at home (it seemed like two years), Malcolm's condition showed no signs of improving. In fact, he was losing ground. Malcolm was losing weight and, each day, struggling harder to breathe. There was no denying the truth. He needed surgery right away.

Soft Hands

My parents, Nancy, Bill, and I were all crowded into Dr. Casteneda's office at Boston Children's Hospital, waiting to meet him. No one spoke. I had a tic in my right eye and a painful, stiff neck.

Malcolm was now in worse shape than when he had first gone to Rhode Island Hospital, at three days old. He was having to face surgery, sick and pathetically weak — just the scenario we had hoped to avoid. All our charts and careful monitoring, all our sleepless nights had been a waste of time.

The door opened and Dr. Casteneda entered, friendly but dignified, with an elegantly straight back and perfect posture. He was dressed in a navy blue, pin-striped suit, his black hair combed back impeccably.

As Patty Romph introduced everyone, Dr. Casteneda bowed in a gracious, Old World way. Instead of taking the seat of power behind his desk, he sat next to my mother. Somehow he managed to combine a sense of expertise and humility. Above all he was real.

"We hope Malcolm has the valve tissue he needs," he said in a soft Spanish accent. (Andrew's mom had told me Dr. Casteneda was from South America, educated in Switzerland, and spoke seven languages.) "We thought we saw some tissue on his echo cardiogram," he said. "But we aren't positive."

He was sure about one thing: Malcolm's heart was too small for a prosthetic valve.

"We'll have to work with the tissue we find," he said. He reached for an envelope from his desk, pulled an antique pen from his suit pocket, and drew a tidy sketch for us of Malcolm's heart and what he hoped to accomplish during the surgery. I was mesmerized by the man's long sinewy fingers, immaculate nails, and expressive hand gestures.

When we stood up to leave, my body felt light and tingly, as though I had just taken off a pair of metal roller skates and was finally moving without friction under my feet. A heaviness rose, like steam, from my chest.

I had done everything I could for my baby. For the next twenty-four hours, I was going off-duty, turning Malcolm over to Dr. Casteneda's flawless care. There was nothing more I could do. Dr. Casteneda extended his hand for me to shake. His was soft, like a newborn's cheek — exactly the sort of hand I wanted touching my baby's heart.

Knocks on the Door

Bill and I are sitting on an unyielding couch in the tiny, ersatz living room. For today, it is our very own holding pen, our space in which to agonize privately and wait for news of Malcolm's surgery.

The place reminds me of the stage set for a soap opera. Garish flowered carpet lies under our feet. Heavy, faux-chintz drapes cover the window. How absurd to have a real window with glass panes and plastic mullions overlooking a hospital corridor. Why not simply hang the curtains over a solid wall or a mural of a pastoral scene? No one inside wants to look out at a shiny, fluorescent hallway filled with rattling gurneys, patients wheeling along their portable IVs, or nurses and interns in their hospital green shower caps and matching scrubs. And no one outside wants to witness the behavior of the stunned, chalk-knuckled parents inside, who pull at their hair and wonder if their child will be alive at day's end.

A gentle knock on the door made my stomach expand and contract, like bellows. It was an OR nurse.

"I just wanted to let you know," she said, "that Malcolm is on the heart and lung machine, and now they will freeze his parts before getting to work."

We thanked her. I looked at my watch: 9:30 A.M.

We sat and waited, dried up and still, like a pair of world-weary mannequins. I reached again for my journal and wrote down the time the nurse had entered and what she had said. Images of frozen body parts and my baby on a steel operating table hovered in my mind.

I sat still, fearing that if I changed positions, even slightly, I might shatter. My breasts ached badly, but I couldn't bring myself to give them relief. What if I were pumping milk at the very moment my son was dying? The thought kept me rigid.

Another knock on the door. I checked my watch and wrote down the time: 11:03 A.M. The nurse again. "Malcolm's mitral valve is deficient, but Dr. Casteneda is going to try to do something."

The next hour seemed interminable. Bill and I stared at nothing and held each other's moist hands.

Another knock: 12:11 P.M. I felt like I'd been in this little room my whole life. The nurse was smiling broadly. What? Why?

"Malcolm is off the heart machine," she announced, triumphant. "His heart is beating on its own."

The solution might be temporary, she explained, a bypass, not a complete fix. But Dr. Casteneda was pleased and would be down shortly to explain everything.

Andrew's mom had been right. They did work miracles in this place!

Bill and I shouted and hugged each other. My milk flowed copiously down my chest. I didn't care.

Now all I wanted was to get out of this hell hole of a room.

Finally, Dr. Casteneda arrived beaming, followed by a crew of clipboard-toting underlings. Wasting no time, he explained that the holes in the atrium and ventricle were easily repaired with heart tissue. The mitral valve leaflets, which released pumped blood from the heart, were frayed and terribly deficient. That's what had caused the enlargement on the right side of the heart: the backed-up blood. There was little valve tissue to work with, so he had taken pericardial tissue from the heart sac and patched the leaflets with that. It seemed to have worked beautifully. As far as Dr. Casteneda knew, no one had ever repaired an infant mitral valve in this way before. Malcolm's was a pioneering procedure.

But we knew, and the doctors reminded us, that the next forty-eight hours would be critical. If he survived the first three days, his chances of a full recovery were excellent.

Post-Op

Bill announced that he was going to take some pictures of Malcolm, to show him when he was grown up. "One of these years," Bill said, beaming, "he can take them in to school for 'show-and-tell.'"

Our son looks like a science experiment. His nose is bandaged to a tube; his arms and legs are dressed in gauze and tied down, as though he's wearing white leotards and tights. A thick tube containing brownish liquid protrudes from his naval; an IV is taped to the side of his head in a freshly shaved patch of hair. Two wires, attached with circular patches of tape, lie against his belly, two more cross his upper chest. There is a catheter running into his penis. A wide dark-red gash of scar bisects his chest.

A nurse fusses with tubes and knobs, her lips pressed hard together, as though she finds our high spirits unwarranted, inappropriate. I'm sure she's wondering who in the world would want to take pictures of such a ghastly sight. And how could parents be ecstatic with their child in such a compromised and precarious state? But she doesn't understand. Our son is ALIVE. He has survived the surgery. Not only that, Dr. Casteneda has FIXED him. The worst is over. We aren't horrified by the tubes and the machines. Not at all. We welcome them: They are going to help our son heal.

Over the doors leading into Cardiac Intensive Care, a sign for parents read: "You Are Not Alone."

At the last hospital, I had been reluctant at first to get involved with other parents. But after those desperate weeks of solitary confinement with Malcolm at home, I was eager to talk to people who might have some idea of what I was going through.

I met Jacob's mom, told her about Malcolm's miracle surgery, and she told me about Jacob. He was a "tetralogy" baby, meaning he had a set of four related heart problems. It wasn't common, but the doctors seemed to know how to cope with this type of defect. Jacob's mom introduced me to all the parents in the lounge. Each had a horror story, but also hope. We drank Cokes and chatted.

Malcolm passed his second full night "post-op." He opened his lids and looked at us, with his bright eyes, as if he fully expected us to be right there and was saying, "Hey, I'm back."

Our son was positively pink, for the first time since his birth. Some minor bleeding into one of his lungs had stopped as mysteriously as it had started. The nurses were weaning him off the respirator. One hung a black-and-white mobile above his head and he stared at it, vigorously kicking his legs. They were beefy legs now, and his once-bony toes and fingers were pudgy. You might almost have been tempted to call him chubby! He was working hard to heal, the nurses told us.

Working hard. I looked down at my small son. In his short life of five weeks, Malcolm had become, in my eyes at least, a hero. I couldn't help but assign grown-up attributes to him — qualities like bravery, self-possession, and wisdom. He was only a baby, but he had endured more pain and trauma than many adults ever do — and he had survived with an uncanny, almost eerie stoicism.

I caught myself singing in the elevator on my way up to Malcolm's floor. Bill and I felt so lucky. Malcolm was thriving. We had incredible support from our friends and families. My parents were keeping everybody updated on Malcolm's progress as well as looking out for Molly. They had even taken her to the vet to be spayed. In about a week, we would get back to Wakefield. Malcolm and Molly would finally meet, and the four of us would be able to take family walks.

The elevator doors slid open. Suddenly, walking toward Malcolm's unit, I heard the dreaded shrill alarm, signaling that a child was in a life-threatening state. It was a call to doctors to drop everything and come, as well as a warning to parents to get the hell out of there, fast. Emergency chest-openings could be done on the spot in each small unit, but were closed to the public. And that included parents.

The heavy metal doors slammed shut in my face just as I arrived. I had no way of knowing if Malcolm was the baby in trouble. Parents who had been inside clustered around the doors. Lydia's mom, one of my new acquaintances, rushed over to me.

"At least I know it's not Lydia," she said. "I was sitting beside her when the alarm sounded, and she was sleeping peacefully."

"It could be Malcolm," I said. "I just got here." I cursed myself for having left briefly to try to sleep.

"Oh dear," Lydia's mom said. "Let's sit down." She led me to a bench and sat beside me. Lydia's mom was Filipino, her husband American. Lydia was their teenage daughter, with beautiful Eurasian looks and a hole in her heart.

As a child, Lydia had undergone two successful cardiac procedures. She had one final surgery left. Her parents, noticing that she was pale and tiring easily, had suggested she go ahead and have it. Lydia refused. Her parents insisted, wanting her to be in top form by the time she left for college, in less than a year.

It was a routine procedure, if you can ever call open-heart surgery routine. The operation went smoothly. But a few days later, as her mother described it, "Lydia's system went berserk." Her body ballooned with fluids; her beautifully sculpted face became round and bumpy. She broke out in a fierce systemic rash and suffered two major seizures. Having trouble breathing, she was back on the respirator.

"Her blood simply didn't want to be rerouted in this new way," Lydia's mom had told me. That was her own personal analysis, and it was as good as anything the doctors could come up with. Lydia's case baffled everyone.

And Lydia, fully conscious and almost an adult, was furious with her parents for having insisted on the surgery.

"We just wanted to operate before she got too weak or sick," Lydia's mom had said. "And now I feel terrible."

"You did the right thing," I told her, clutching her hand. "What else could you have done? She was failing."

One of the huge doors opened and Cheryl, Malcolm's new day nurse, came out. Cheryl was particularly fond of Malcolm. She'd told Bill that she had a dream about him. "He's so handsome," she said. She had nicknamed him "Hollywood Henderson" on account of his star quality and the breakthrough surgery. Now she was headed in my direction, her curly brown hair (that Malcolm loved to reach for), bobbing gently as she walked. I felt the blood draining from my face. Lydia's mom squeezed my hand.

"It's not Malcolm," Cheryl said. "I knew you hadn't been inside and I wanted to let you know."

I exhaled deeply. Lydia's mom wrapped her arm around my shoulder.

Cheryl walked over to a couple who had just arrived the night before. Their newborn daughter had been operated on in the middle of the night. Now they were both leaning against the wall by the elevators.

The rest of us looked down, not wanting to seem intrusive. Cheryl said something we couldn't hear and the mother slumped against her husband. Cheryl helped the man hold his wife up. She said something else and he shook his head vehemently and said, "No." His voice was loud and angry. He pressed the elevator button again and again. The doors opened and the two of them got on, the woman sobbing and pounding on the man's chest. The shiny elevator doors closed.

No one moved or spoke. We all knew it could have been one of us.

Before Malcolm was born, I had assumed that hospitals were institutions of applied wisdom and healing. If you became sick, you went to the hospital and a specialist cured you. It was simple, reliable. I didn't know that even the best doctors in the world are stymied by mysteries, that after losing battles they were convinced they had won, doctors threw up their hands in defeat, without a clue. It didn't get through to me that people died every day in hospitals, even babies. I wasn't aware that survival was dictated as much by dumb luck as anything else.

One week after surgery all the tubes and paraphernalia are gone. I can hold and feed Malcolm again. His heart is pumping smoothly and he is breathing comfortably on his own. He no longer grunts!

Doctors paraded through our area. They clasped our hands in affirming shakes and marveled out loud at the success of their colleague, shaking their heads and scratching their chins at his genius (and by affiliation their own). One doctor told me Malcolm might be on the cover of *Time* some day, the first man in the world to have successfully undergone this particular surgery.

Our friend Debbie from California was in town on business and came by the hospital to visit us. She brought Malcolm a large Gund teddy bear and an outfit for an eighteen-month-old.

"Something to grow into," she announced. Debbie was a large, full-bodied woman with a booming voice. She was earthy, motherly. Her visit was like a spell of thawing spring after a frigid winter. She smiled and cooed at Malcolm and he smiled and cooed back. He held her finger. She treated him as if he was a normal baby. I was finally beginning to believe he was.

As I attempted to talk to Debbie about mutual friends and worldly issues, I felt out of shape, only dimly remembering the person I had been — before Malcolm. The talk with other hospital parents was always about meds, monitors, and methods. I hadn't had a "normal" conversation in weeks.

Debbie took Bill and me to dinner at a restaurant in the Copley Plaza Hotel in downtown Boston. I watched the people sitting around us. They were chatting, sipping wine, and laughing; their bright teeth matched the white linen tablecloths. I stared at the art on the walls, stroked the linen napkins, and, like a dog, relished the smells of my gourmet meal. I felt like a prisoner on parole. Life in the hospital is awesomely devoid of texture and detail and material comfort.

I sensed I was traveling back in time to another life, to an era when people went out and had fun together and were unburdened. Life could actually be carefree! I was resurfacing, emerging from a dark hole, blinking back into the light after a tortuous journey through the underworld.

During dessert, I looked over at Bill through the candlelight and remembered that the first time I met him, I had known instantly that he was going to be the father of my children. It was one of those classic intuitive flashes. You hear about them, but you don't believe it's possible, until it happens to you. My next thought had been that I deeply loved this man I had just met and that we would spend the rest of our lives together. He was my soulmate, my other half. Where did these weird, sudden insights come from, I wondered. Now, I watched him talk proudly about our son's tenacious struggle and victory.

"Soon we'll be home with Malcolm," Bill said to me, reaching for my hand. A whole new world was opening up for us.

At the hospital we no longer had to suit up and disinfect ourselves before entering Malcolm's unit. He was stable and we were scheduled to move out of Intensive Care into a regular room for a day or two before going home.

But I was still nervous. Were Malcolm's respirations a little higher or was I imagining things? I was going to have to learn to relax. I tried to brush away my concern. But I couldn't.

Patty Romph was right. No one knew our son better than Bill and I did. And I had a hunch now that something was different; I could just feel it, even though the resident in charge brushed off my concern.

I insisted that the resident page Dr. Casteneda. Malcolm spit up his food and his respirations rose dramatically. A nurse started him on an IV. Dr. Casteneda scheduled another echo cardiogram, which showed that his heart was enlarged again.

A crowd of white coats assembled around Malcolm. I watched as Dr. Lang, a long-haired cardiologist who always wore black jeans and reminded Bill and me of Art Garfunkel, listened to my baby's heart. He yanked the stethoscope out of his ears and turned away from me.

"Damn," he said. "Not this baby."

I couldn't believe that we had just toasted Malcolm's good health with a friend over dinner. We should have known better. Cardiac units, like combat zones, were ruled by cosmic tricksters.

Malcolm is crying miserably but I can't hold him. His lungs are filling up and it would be too dangerous. I sit by him and rock in my chair, occasionally getting up to rub his head and whisper in his ear. Tears trickle from my cheeks to his.

I think a dybbuk has invaded my son's soul. His behavior and body movements are completely unrecognizable. He thrashes from side to side and emits pathetic, weak laments. The sight and smell of me seem to make him worse. I try to comfort him, but he will have none of me. He won't hold my pinkie. I sense he knows he is dying and he's furious.

Dr. Casteneda scheduled surgery for the next morning. No one seemed hopeful about Malcolm's prospects.

The morning of surgery was rainy and dismal. We stopped on our way into the hospital to buy coffee from a cheerful street vendor, who was always stationed under his colorful umbrella. We had become regulars. He began making his usual jokes, but after looking at my face, stopped midsentence and nervously adjusted his cap. He recognized the look; he had probably seen it before on the faces of other frantic parents making last-ditch pilgrimages into the hospital.

On our way to an OR waiting room, we passed Lydia's mom, standing at the end of the corridor. I lifted my hand in a feeble wave.

Having waited for a sign from me, she now rushed down the hall. "Oh, Carol!" Lydia's mom hugged me, the way she had so many times over the past weeks. "Everybody in the lounge is praying for you today."

I thanked her. It wasn't until later that I realized Lydia's mom had called me "Carol," not "Malcolm's mom."

Malcolm was breathing hard, but seemed calm, resigned. Perhaps they had given him an anesthetic. I was too tired and scared to check his chart.

I kissed my son one more time in the hollow of his pale cheek. I memorized his face.

"You can take him now," I told the doctor.

Malcolm was sucking hard on his pacifier. His bright eyes darted around the room, taking it all in — the nurses whispering in the corner, the lights, the shiny IV pole he could see his reflection in.

The doctor wrapped his big hands around Malcolm and carefully picked him up. I assume this is a courtesy to parents — carrying the child rather than wheeling him away, like a ham in a grocery cart. As a final image, a baby held in human arms might be easier to live with.

Malcolm and the doctor disappeared though double swinging doors.

"Curtains"

A nurse knocked. Bill and I were stationed in yet another "pretend" living room, this one decorated in fake William Morris paisleys. Earlier, Cheryl had told me Dr. Casteneda had a few tricks up his sleeve, a few ideas for ways to save Malcolm.

"What if they all failed?" I had asked. "It would be 'curtains,' right?"

"That's right," she said, not meeting my gaze. "Curtains."

The OR nurse knocked and reported that Malcolm was on the heart and lung machine. As soon as she finished speaking, she bowed quickly out of the room.

Unlike the last surgery, when an OR nurse regularly updated us, this time no one knocked. Hours passed.

Finally, the knock came.

"Come in," Bill said, his voice weak and breathless.

Dr. Casteneda walked in, alone. Although impeccably dressed, as always, the man's chest seemed to have caved in, his suit stripes no longer made perfect perpendicular angles to the ground. He looked almost fuzzy, like an aging movie star in an old black and white film. His eyes had receded into their sockets, as though in retreat from what he had seen or was about to witness. I felt sorry for him, having to tell us.

He walked across the room and sat down beside me. The surgeon took my hand in his. "I'm so sorry," he said, shaking his head and looking down. "We lost him."

For one of the only times since Malcolm's birth, Bill began to cry — ragged, heaving tears.

I didn't. It was Bill's turn. Finally, his optimism and manly courage were no longer necessary, no longer useful. He had persisted in a spirit of hope, determined to counter my black fear. Like a marathoner, he had paced steadily through the dark ordeal, trying to light a path for both of us. Now he could hurl the torch into the void and succumb to his own long-suppressed grief.

Still holding my hand, Dr. Casteneda explained what had happened. The pressure of the pumping blood had destroyed the earlier repair, blown the patch right off the valve. They couldn't try that again and a prosthetic valve, their only other hope, wouldn't fit.

Knowing his duties with us were over, I waited for him to explain further or to get up and leave. But he didn't budge. He just sat beside me, holding my hand.

Dr. Lang knocked and came in. He didn't sit down.

"I'm so sorry," he said, moving from one foot to the other. "Malcolm was such a special little fighter."

Bill shook his head, still crying. My eyes remained dry. I felt nothing at all. And knowing nothing at all about the numb, dumb state called shock, I assumed everything was truly over, including my emotional life — that I wouldn't feel anything, ever again. I studied Dr. Lang's face, noticing for the first time a deep crease across his forehead.

Acutely alert, I looked around the room; everything seemed sharply focused, like a superrealist photograph. Dr. Lang looked at the ground. Dr. Casteneda sat, holding my hand, his head down. Was he praying? The air was getting heavy with the weight of these men. I knew they were disappointed by their surgical failure, but they also seemed genuinely sad, as though Malcolm were someone they had known well and cared deeply about.

"If there's anything I can do for either of you," Dr. Lang said, breaking the silence, "don't hesitate to call me. Anything."

Dr. Casteneda let go of my hand and stood up. "You both did everything you possibly could for Malcolm," he said. "And more."

"So did you," I said.

The men headed for the door.

"Wait," I said, an idea crashing into my brain, like a rock through a glass window. "What about Malcolm's or-

61

gans? Could we donate some of them, maybe his liver or his kidneys, to another baby?"

This possibility filled me with an almost hysterical enthusiasm. But I could tell by their despondent faces that these doctors had seen this before, parents grasping for some larger meaning and purpose.

"That's a kind offer," Dr. Lang said. "But Malcolm was too sick."

They turned toward the door.

"But what about his eyes?" I asked. "Those perfect eyes?"

"I'm sorry," Dr. Lang said, looking back at me. "But no."

They were heading out the door.

"Wait!" Bill said. He had regained his composure. Both men turned and looked at him. "What about all of Carol's frozen milk in the ICU? Couldn't some baby use that?"

Lang shook his head. "Sorry. Not that either."

I shrugged my shoulders.

"We're all so sorry," Dr. Casteneda said.

Heads down, the doctors turned their backs to us and left the room, careful to close the door behind them.

Bill moved over and sat by me on the couch, taking my hand the way Dr. Casteneda had. What would happen now? No one would knock; there would be no news to knock about. The room seemed calm, almost balmy, like the hushed atmosphere of a hurricane's eye.

So we talked. About how hard Malcolm had fought for his life, how brave he had been, how he had known he was going to die that day, and how peaceful, yet attentive he had been when the doctor finally took him away for the last time. Our conversation seemed oddly like small talk, the kind you make when you're waiting on a bench for a bus, chatting with the other riders about the weather and road conditions. You know you're going to have this same conversation over and over again, for years to come, as long as you ride the bus.

I felt like the Teflon parent. Nothing was sticking to me; I was a tabula rasa, a blank book. Then, with a jolt, I remembered something. There were other parents, stuck in some public area, who desperately needed this private grieving room.

"We've got to get out of here right away," I said, pulling Bill up. "I just know someone is waiting to get in here."

I opened the door. We blinked at the bright hospital corridor, not knowing which way to go. We started in one direction and then turned abruptly and headed the other way, like those beetles who live under rocks and scurry this way and that when you turn their stone over and expose them to the light.

Cheryl and Michele (Malcolm's favorite night nurse) approached us. They must have been waiting somewhere, watching the door for our exit. What was Michele doing here, I wondered? Her shift ended at seven in the morning and it was midafternoon.

"I wanted to tell you in person how sorry I am," Michele said. Malcolm was so special . . . to everyone." Michele's eyes filled with tears. I put my arms out and she hugged me.

"If you want to see Malcolm," Cheryl said, "we can arrange to have his body brought to the hospital chapel."

"We'll think about it and let you know," Bill said. We thanked them for everything they had done. Both women were wiping their eyes.

I thought about the pressure these nurses lived under — it was enough to flatten the average mortal. Disaster blew regularly through a cardiac ward. Successful repairs suddenly backfired. Babies died. Parents deconstructed.

Another voice: "Mr. and Mrs. Henderson!"

We turned around and saw an elderly old-school type with a stiff spine and hair drawn back severely in a no-nonsense bun: a social worker.

"I've been looking for you both," she said, with proper-Bostonian inflections. I wondered if she were a volunteer, a blue-blood out to do her deed for humanity, an aged "candy-striper."

"I'm terribly sorry," she said.

I felt empty, as still and clear as a glass of water. Bill told the woman what Cheryl had said about viewing Malcolm's body.

"Don't go see him," the social worker advised, her voice taking on a sharp, almost imperious edge. She pointed like a traffic cop at an automatic sliding glass exit far down the corridor.

"There's the door." She pinched my sleeve in her hand and gave me a little pull in the direction of the door. "Just leave the hospital. I always tell people it's better that way."

This woman wasn't our assigned social worker and we had only talked with her once before. Neither of us had particularly enjoyed our previous contact with her. She seemed unyielding, rigid, almost mean. But she was trained to know, at a time like this, the best course of action. Wasn't she? I thought of Malcolm, torn down the middle and still cold from the surgical deep-freezing. What was the point of seeing him — all blue and cold and *gone*? During our time in the hospital, I had purposefully avoided the chaplain's earnest gaze; and I had stayed out of the in-house chapel. That was a place where believers went to pray for their offspring's recovery and, when technology and miracles failed, to hug their dead children. The thought of entering that solemn sanctuary sent a spurt of acid up my windpipe — the first visceral response I had experienced in what seemed like hours.

I wondered, fleetingly, if the act of seeing Malcolm's body was important, psychologically. My mother, I knew, would agree with the social worker. "Don't risk upsetting yourself," she would have said. And also, having never seen a dead body, I wasn't sure I wanted to start now — with my own son's.

Furthermore, my thoughts were jolted by another horrifying possibility: What if other people were in the chapel with their dead babies? I had observed and absorbed so much of other people's grief already. I couldn't take any more.

Another thought rose up, like a freak tsunami in an otherwise calm surf: If I held Malcolm, how would I ever be able to give him up, turn him back in, like a library book. My son, the unfinished story. How could I say to a nurse: "Here! Take him!" knowing it was for keeps. If I saw him, I'd have to shove him into my purse and rush out of the hospital with my bundle. And then what? Keep him . . . forever?

I tried to push my thoughts down and away, but a new idea surfaced. What if I made a scene and lost control in public, like the native in James Michener's *Hawaii*, who plucked out his own eye with a stick and tossed it onto the grave of his beloved wife, while the missionaries watched in horror.

I looked at the prim social worker, with her long neck and round-collared blouse, clasped safely at the neck with a small gold pin. She wouldn't want me to "lose it" in the chapel. How vulgar and inappropriate a show of hysterics would be, especially coming from a good, buttoned-up WASP like me. I was one of *her* kind. She wanted to spare me the possibility of embarrassing myself, and her, in public.

"Just leave." She said it emphatically. I wondered how long we had been standing there with her.

I glanced down the hall. A slant of late autumn sun seemed to beckon from outside the hospital's exit door. Having lived under fluorescent lights for weeks, I ached to pass through that automatic slider. I would be free! I could skip and jump! Our ordeal was over! Never again would I pad the halls of this wretched place, my guts in my throat.

Bill and I followed the social worker's directions. We walked down the hall and out the door. We didn't know any better. We didn't know the importance of saying good-bye.

Hours of Lead

How often will the vast emptiness astonish me
like a complete novelty and make me say,
"I never realized my loss until this moment?"

C. S. Lewis, *A Grief Observed*

Shock

The sliding glass doors delivered us into a dazzling sunny afternoon. What a contrast to the predawn gloom we had arrived in, when a steady, cold rain had drummed against the sidewalk and halos of fog encircled the street lights. Now, the air was crisp and clear. Baroque cloud banks rolled across the sky, like moving mountains; the sun poured down in golden, radiant beams. I was convinced the turn in weather was an omen, a miracle: The hospital hostages were free at last! I smiled and waved at the vendor under his umbrella, flushed with pleasure that I would never have to buy another cup of coffee from him.

67

We walked back to the Children's Inn, where we'd been headquartered, past the two ebullient "Up with People" staff members behind the front desk. Instead of their usual eager faces and jovial greetings, they both suddenly looked sober and turned their eyes away from us. Somebody must have told them or maybe our faces and body language said it all. We didn't speak to them, just nodded in passing. And they nodded in return.

I surprised myself by telling Bill I wanted to make the call to my parents. All along, he had been the correspondent, endlessly reciting his hopeful refrain about the great care and the amazing powers of modern surgery. Only three days earlier his words had resonated with promise.

I knew my parents had been holed up all day, waiting for this call. I could almost see my father puttering around the house, slamming drawers too hard, and my mother clutching her Xeroxed copies of pages from the *Book of Common Prayer*, her lips moving in desperate entreaty.

My father answered the phone.

"It's over, Daddy," I said, matter-of-factly. "Malcolm didn't make it."

"Oh, sweetie," my father said, his voice cracking. "I'm . . . we're so. . . ."

I could hear him start to break down. Still, I felt nothing. Why was he crying? I wondered. Didn't he know it was *over*? Trying to cheer him up, I described the view out the hotel window. I told him about the magnificent sunset, the purple clouds edged in bright pink, the amber ball of sun about to plunge out of sight.

"Malcolm's out there somewhere," I said. "He's in that incredible sky."

There was a brief silence on the other end of the line.

"You sound very strong, dearie," he stammered.

"I am," I said, feeling like the Bionic Woman.

I heard whimpering and whispering in the background.

"Your mother can't come to the phone right now."

"That's all right," I said, knowing it wasn't our family's style to deal directly with dire matters. "I understand. I'll call you again later when we know our plans."

Bill had to deliver a writing job to a production studio in Jamaica Plain, a nearby suburb. Luckily, he had finished the work earlier in the week, before Malcolm's precipitous fall. Not wanting to stay alone in the hotel room, I went along for the car ride. As soon as we pulled out onto the main avenue, an endless sea of brake lights loomed before us. Rush hour. In recent weeks, traffic jams had delayed many of our arrivals, making us late for critical meetings with doctors and stressing us almost to the breaking point. Seeing the gridlock, I panicked. How would we ever get back in time?

Straining forward in my seat and stamping my feet, I scanned the urban landscape, searching for a way out of the traffic. Horns honked. The side streets were jammed with stopped cars. We were definitely stuck.

And then it hit me: So what? I didn't have to race back to Malcolm's side. He wasn't crying for me. Doctors weren't poking him or waiting to discuss the latest turn in his health with us. I could sit in this traffic for hours, for days, for months—and not miss anything. Malcolm wasn't there. He wasn't anywhere. I was free. I turned on the car radio, scanned the dial until I found some classical music, and sat back.

We parked on the street a few doors past the production studio. Walking, Bill and I held hands, smiling and nodding at people we passed on the sidewalk. Wouldn't they all be surprised if they knew our situation — only two hours earlier, this nice couple's son had died. I felt as if I were hiding a heinous crime, like a character in a Dostoyevsky novel. Thinking about my deceit made me lightheaded.

We chatted cheerfully with the folks in the office, telling them nothing and leaving quickly. Eventually, these same people would know the truth. They would scratch their heads and say to each other: "From talking with them then, I never would have believed their baby had just died."

We decided to go to Harvard Square for a leisurely dinner. I wouldn't have to find a pay phone and call in, my stomach pushing on my lungs, or leave the meal half-eaten to dash back to a crisis at the hospital. During one such dinner, I remembered, I had pumped my breasts in the restaurant's cramped bathroom and stored the milk in the ice bucket, with our bottle of wine. Now, we had all night to eat and drink and browse in the bookstores.

While stopped at a red light, I watched a square-shouldered, short man cross in front of the car. He was smiling broadly. Who knew? He might have just learned he had a terminal disease, with three months left to live. Or maybe he was remembering the riotous sex he'd had the night before, with someone other than his wife. A tall woman in a flowing wool coat and high heels walked by briskly, as though on her way to an important engagement. Maybe she was only on her way to that pub across the road to drink herself under the table. You couldn't tell a thing about people by watching them going about their daily tasks.

We parked on the far side of Radcliffe Yard and headed across the tree-covered campus green toward the restaurants and shops, our old stomping grounds. Having lived in Cambridge the first three years of our married life, we knew the area well; we'd spent hours poking around in the dusty, second-hand bookstores and drinking coffee in dimly lit cafes. Bill had been a musician then, and his band played regularly in Harvard Square. The modern dance company I had performed with was headquartered in a church right off the Cambridge Common.

That was all *before*, I said to myself, as we walked along the brick path holding hands. Before what? I couldn't remember. The familiar chimes of a steeple clock filled the air, announcing the hour in seven loud bells. Before what? I asked myself again. Before what?

Before we had a child.

Out of nowhere, I heard a woman screaming. Something terrible was happening. Several seconds — maybe it was minutes — passed before I realized the shrieks were coming from my mouth.

My son was dead. This wasn't one of those wrenching narratives I had read about in the morning paper — a tale of hope and miracles and sudden death — that had destroyed someone else's life; this tragedy had happened to *me*. The dam of numb denial had broken. My shrill cries echoed sharply off the cold brick walls enclosing Radcliffe Yard. The stately buildings seemed to be gazing down at me, aghast, unaccustomed to hearing such raw, feral emotion.

Suddenly, I seemed to leave my body and look down at myself from somewhere high above me. I saw an unkempt woman, raging like Rochester's crazy wife. Bill had one arm around her shoulder. His other arm made a diagonal across her front, from her waist to her shoulder, like a seat belt or one of those "no smoking" signs. With sideways, crablike shuffles, Bill moved the woman along the path.

I swooped down, back into my ragged frame and felt Bill's arms around me. He guided my body firmly and slowly in the direction from which we had come. It was a good thing he was holding me; if I'd been able to bolt, I would have hurled myself at those brick walls and ripped at them, brick by brick, with my bare hands.

People were staring. Whispering in my ear that everything was okay, Bill ushered me into the car and strapped me in. My front was drenched in clammy breast milk, all the way down to my knees.

Bill drove us back to the Children's Inn and led me to our room. There was a phone message from Patty Romph. Bill called her back and stayed on the phone for a long time. I paced the room, moaning in a kind of low growl. I wanted to die, right there on the carpet. If my son had to be dead, I had to get dead to be with him. Dying no longer held any fear for me. Malcolm had done it — so could I. Patty asked to speak to me, but, being my mother's daughter, I couldn't bring myself to come to the phone.

After Bill hung up, he told me something Patty had said to him. She had told us both once before, but she wanted Bill to remind me: "Remember," she said. "You will always be Malcolm's parents and he will always be your son."

Bill made me stop pacing and lie down. I closed my eyes and saw my nipples as Fourth of July sparklers, sending shoots of fiery pain whirling out across my chest. He put hot washcloths on them and gave me three aspirins. Nothing seemed to help the pain. He drew me a hot bath. Remembering Dr. Lang's offer of assistance, Bill called and asked him if there was anything he could prescribe to dry up my milk. Lang had nothing to suggest and seemed annoyed at being asked about something as mundane as sore breasts. He had moved on, of course, to other patients and other families. Our story had entered the realm of stats and figures: Henderson — failed lesion. Dead file. Dr. Lang was finished with us.

Bill slammed the phone down, furious with the doctor's unspoken message. "You're asking *me* this? Try one of the nurses." And he was furious at his own utter powerlessness. His son was gone, his wife was hysterical and in acute physical pain, and there wasn't a thing he could do about any of it.

That night, I tossed and turned in bed, feeling like I was being stabbed again and again in my breasts. Hard cones of pain, they seemed to carry their own rage. Images from the ICU flashed through my brain like a gruesome slide show I couldn't turn off: CLICK . . . to the baby with the stomach outside . . . to Lydia's furious face . . . to Malcolm writhing in rage.

I rubbed my eyes, trying to make the images go away. But they were relentless, breaking over me the way a mean surf pounds a beach. Finally, I cried myself to sleep.

An hour later my sobs woke us both. I had dreamt about Malcolm's death, in superrealist detail, exactly as it had happened. All over again, I unballed his little fist's grasp on my finger, kissed his cheek, and watched him get carried away for the last time, sucking on his pacifier, his bright eyes taking it all in. I saw Dr. Casteneda's sunken

73

face when he came in to see us after surgery. I relived his taking my hand. All of it was raw reality, far more painful than a nightmare I could wake up from and say, "Thank God it was only a dream."

Funeral Parlor

Malcolm died yesterday afternoon. Period. Will writing down the facts make them easier to accept? No. Not now.

I'm sitting on the edge of the hotel bed, rocking back and forth and clutching my journal. Bill is packing us up to leave. The phone rings. We don't answer it. When the ringing stops, he calls the front desk.

"We aren't taking calls," he says. The desk people tell him it was our friends Bill and Danice from California. They brought their little girl Lilah to visit us when I was pregnant. Lilah felt my huge belly and told me she had picked out a special red terrycloth bear — "for your baby."

It's not yet eight o'clock, our time. Bill and Danice must have heard already and gotten up at five o'clock, hoping to reach us before we leave this morning. How brave they are. I've never had the courage to put in an "I'm so sorry," call, even to a good friend. I didn't write to Sue when her mother died, convincing myself it was because I didn't want to remind her about her mother's death. As if she was thinking about anything else! What really kept me from writing was cowardice and fear. I couldn't face Sue's grief or the possibility of my own mother dying. . . .

I've got to get out of this hotel room. The walls, the furniture, the air are contaminated with grief.

The elderly social worker had recommended a funeral parlor near the hospital. She had told us several times to make sure and mention her name to the funeral director. I had never set foot in a funeral home, but they all seemed to look the same, at least from the outside. All over America, I had seen the tell-tale landscaping: postage-stamp lawns and neatly edged privet hedges. Mortuaries always seemed to be in older houses, plunked down right in the middle of urban areas. Were these houses the only surviving structures from an earlier era, before the residential neighborhood had been razed for strip malls? Or did they still build them to look that way? This one was nestled between and dwarfed by a deluxe new gas station and a massive office complex. Inside, the unctuously somber tone of the foyer made my stomach drop to my boots and my heart ache. Plush imitation oriental carpet lined the front hall. It was yet another phony habitat. Out of a side door, a tall, gray man appeared. He looked and smelled like a cigarette. I'd be a chain smoker, too, if I had his job.

"Good morning," he said.

He put out a bony hand at the end of a long, thin arm. He reminded me of one of those plastic stick figures used in sculpture classes, the kind that could be bent, like pipe cleaners, into all sorts of contorted positions. I extended my arm to shake his hand, felt a shooting pain in my right breast, and grimaced.

"I'm so sorry, Mrs. Henderson."

He shook Bill's hand, led us into an illusion of a living room, and shut the door. The decor was meant to be sober and cozy, but there was no air in the room. I felt like I was trapped in an elevator. I wanted to scream. My breasts were going to burst. If only I could paw them off my chest. I longed to leave my body again, the way I had in Radcliffe Yard. I wanted to sail away from myself and never come back.

Bill did all the talking for us and filled out the death certificate. The man told us Malcolm's ashes couldn't be sent across state lines without first being sealed in a proper container. It was a state or federal law. Whatever it was, it sounded like a racket to me. If we wanted to wait several days, we could pick up his ashes ourselves at the crematorium. Otherwise, we had to buy an urn and have them sent.

He showed us several styles and spoke fervently about each line, as though these were china patterns to be shown off at a wedding reception. I tried to imagine the scene: "And here on the mantel," we would say to friends, "is the lovely Corinthian-columned design number 84, holding our son's ashes."

The whole concept struck me as ludicrous and exploitative. We picked the cheapest, simplest one.

"Wouldn't you like your urn engraved?" the funeral parlor man asked. I could tell he was disappointed we had gone for the bottom of the line. But he smiled anyway, in a way that reminded me of Art Linkletter.

"Sure," Bill said. "Engrave it."

"What do you want it to say?" Bill asked me.

I wanted to slap myself. Was this really happening? What *was* happening? I felt the man's eyes on me.

"Malcolm," I said. "Write Malcolm on it."

"Is that all?" the man asked, his eyebrows going up. (You paid by the word.)

"That's all," I said.

The man reminded us that Malcolm would be cremated at Mount Auburn Crematorium, a most reputable operation and one of the largest in the country.

In an instant, I saw an image of Malcolm's fine hair catching flame and rising in an updraft, the soft peach fuzz on his sculpted shoulders sparking. Wait a minute, I thought. Someone was actually going to stick my son in an oven and *burn* him. I tried to blink away the image. I heard his bones cracking in the blaze, those long runner's legs catching like kindling.

I had to get out of that room.

"Excuse me," I said, rising. I tripped across the thick carpeted hall and pushed open the heavy outside door, breathing deeply, my nostrils stinging at the rush of cold air. The motion of my ribs made my breasts ache again. And then the image returned — my son's body, ablaze. I plopped down on the cement steps and put my head between my legs. Blood pounded through my temples; hot pain tore at my chest.

I tried to reason with myself. Malcolm wasn't in his body anymore. His spirit was soaring somewhere far away, released finally from that scrawny frame, with its enlarged organs, spent lungs, and the dark scab down its middle. Bill and I had discussed the matter several times: We would rather our son be cremated than buried. Where would we bury him? We would want the grave to be close to where we lived. But we moved so often. Who even knew how long we would stay in Boston, once we moved there? A little box of ashes could go anywhere we went. For itinerant types like us, cremation seemed the only choice.

Where was Malcolm? I couldn't believe he was gone, that he had simply vanished off the face of the Earth.

Bill followed me out the door, leaving the mortician standing in the foyer. Undoubtedly the man was relieved to be rid of us, unresponsive cheapskates who didn't appreciate his distinguished collection of urns.

The Lounge

With all our business in Boston finished, we were free to leave town. Our next destination was the house in Rhode Island. There we would find the paraphernalia, all that remained of our child — the bottles of meds standing in a row, like hopeful soldiers inside the refrigerator door. There would be the milk-stained sleepers we hadn't had time to wash before rushing to the hospital, the piles of gifts people had sent, and the boxes of borrowed hand-me-downs (enough clothes and sizes to dress Malcolm for years). It would all be there waiting for us, along with the unwired lighting fixtures and the unfinished paint jobs.

As we were headed toward the Turnpike, I became increasingly anxious.

"I think I've got to go back to the hospital," I said. "I don't feel right about leaving this state without saying good-bye to the other parents."

"Are you sure you want to go back in there?" Bill asked. I could tell he was surprised. So was I. It was so unlike me, or anyone in my family, to *choose* to endure such an uncomfortable scene.

"Yes," I said. "I need to go."

Bill took the next exit and we turned in the direction of Children's Hospital.

I walked through the glass doors, bewildered that I was again walking into the deadly maze of this awful building. Hadn't I vowed never to return?

I entered our parents' lounge. As soon as she saw me, Lydia's mother approached quickly and took my hand.

"I'm so sorry," she said. There were tears in her eyes.

We hugged each other. My breasts throbbed violently. I wondered if she could feel their fury.

"How's Lydia?" I asked, biting my lip, trying to keep myself together.

"She had another seizure last night," she said. The ever-changing wrinkles around her eyes made a sudden tic-tac-toe pattern across her cheekbones. "I missed you."

I squeezed her hand. I had been there during Lydia's last seizure. The alarm had sounded and we'd all had to leave the area, even Lydia's mom. Breathless, we had sat, holding hands like we were now, waiting for news.

Lydia, I was afraid, would be next.

Several parents came over and spoke to me.

"I couldn't leave town without saying good-bye to you guys," I said, my voice dry and shaky. If we had all met at a party, we most likely wouldn't have had two words for each other. For that matter, we would never have been invited to the same party. In the outside world, we had nothing in common — here, hovering over our kids' sick beds, we had everything. These people knew the agony of waiting for news from the OR; they knew how rudely and randomly the Reaper tore through this place, snatching children; they knew how exhausted I was. And yet now I was free to leave for good, a fate none of them wanted if it meant going empty-handed. They also knew that, at any moment, what had happened to me could happen to them.

"There are groups, you know, for parents who have lost kids," Lydia's mom said. "You might want to look into one of those."

If I joined any group, I thought, it would be these people I would want in it. I wouldn't have to retell my tale — they knew it already. We had shared the same nurses, the same doctors, the same lounge. They had all known Malcolm; some of them had even held him, a privilege denied my own sisters because he died before they had a chance to visit.

"I wouldn't want to join just any group," I said.

"But," Jacob's mom said, "ultimately, all parents who lose a child end up in the same place, no matter how it happens. They end up without their kid. You'd have that in common."

"Maybe you could find a cardiac group," said Lydia's mom. "They would have known the same type of hell."

My shoulders rose and then sagged. Maybe.

I sat down, looked out the window at the brick wall, and wondered how many hours I had spent in this room with these people. Everyone else sat down too. They were waiting. But my wait was over. What was I doing here? Bill was in the car, probably worrying about what had become of me. He hadn't known this side of hospital life — the round-the-clock nervous waiting, punctuated by breaks out in the lounge with the other parents. He had come to the hospital to see Malcolm and to interrogate the doctors, but had missed completely this grim camaraderie.

While I hung out in the lounge, he'd been back at the hotel, trying to concentrate on some script he was writing or across town at a production studio, directing a voice-over session. One dad was on a paid leave from work and could hang around day and night. For a freelancer, there are no paid leaves. I knew; I hadn't earned a cent in weeks.

Bill had told me he had mixed feelings about not being able to spend every minute at the hospital. He was relieved, almost exhilarated, to escape the stressful environment. But he was dogged by guilt for feeling that way.

"And no matter what I'm doing," he had said, "there is this bizarre sense of unreality about my life. When I'm talking to clients or sitting in a meeting, I feel like an actor playing a role."

He also thought that if he'd been there more he might have been able to exert some control over Malcolm's situation, might have been able to make things better somehow. But we both knew that the whole idea of control in a cardiac ward was an illusion.

Bill's absence had forced me to be more aggressive with doctors, to ask more questions, to demand attention for my son. Had Bill been there all the time, I would have hidden behind him, let him be on the front line. My friends from the hospital, these people I was sitting with, had helped me learn how to fight.

I knew I had to get up and go. But I didn't. I couldn't. I just sat there, unable to tear myself away from this odd lot of parents who had been thrown together by fate or bad luck — by both.

"Well, I guess I'd better get going," I said finally, knowing I would never see any of these friends again. On my way out, Lydia's mother squeezed my hand one last time.

"I need a miracle now," she whispered.

"I know," I said, hoping hers would be a true miracle, not like ours.

I walked out of the lounge, down the sterile corridor, and out the sliding glass doors, heartbroken at having to leave this place I had hated so much.

Neighbors

Heading south past Providence, I thought of the times over the past two months I had made this trip, aching with fear, longing to get back to my baby. The imaginary cord that bound Malcolm to me had unfurled reluctantly whenever I had to leave him and stayed taut and steely, yanking on me, until I returned to him. Now, as we drove into Wakefield, I realized the cord had been severed; I was in free-fall, like a topsy-turvy figure in a Chagall painting.

Bill opened the door to the house. Gingerly, we stepped inside. The first impression of clutter and haste made me think of a theater set for a melodrama about sudden evacuation. Piles of mail and newspapers jammed the mail slot and spilled across the floor. A half-drunk baby bottle, the breast milk yellowed, stood on the stairwell; rumpled infant sleepers littered the furniture. The house was oppressively still. Where were the workers, the dog, the grandparents? Where was the baby?

I sat down on the familiar couch, my laboring spot, and stared at nothing. Bill sat beside me and thumbed through a few pieces of mail. There were several hospital and doctor bills. He didn't open them. He did open a hand-addressed envelope bearing a congratulatory note that read, "Hooray, it's a boy!"

"Maybe I should go get us something to eat," he said, putting the card back in the envelope and the rest of the mail down on the floor. We hadn't had a square meal in days.

"Yeah," I said. "That's a good idea."

"Will you be okay here alone?"

"Better here than downtown where I might see somebody I know," I said. I knew I wouldn't be able to handle encounters with anyone now. What would I say? How would I behave? I didn't have a clue and didn't want to find out.

"I'll only be a few minutes," Bill said. "Don't try to read the mail or anything."

After he left, I drifted around the house like a ghost, gazing at the evidence of the life I once lived—the kitchen counter littered with used syringes, the freezer full of breast milk. Upstairs, in Malcolm's room, I sat heavily on the cot Mother had bought me. The crib and changing table were still raised at one end to ease Malcolm's breathing. Somehow I couldn't believe that this drama had actually played out. But tangible proof loomed everywhere around me, even in my body. My incision ached, my breasts throbbed, and my eyes burned from exhaustion.

I know I should try to tidy up, but I can't find the strength to rise up off the cot. I reach down and pick up a green terrycloth sleeper from the floor; Malcolm's scent still lingers in it. How can I ever wash it? When Erica's sister died in that plane crash twenty years ago, Mrs. Hendricks left her daughter's room exactly as it was at the time of her death. The brush on the bureau held the girl's hair, an unfinished book lay open, spine down, on the bedside table. The door to the bedroom was always open. On a dare, Erica and I rushed in there, touched the bedspread, and ran out again, shaking. I'm sure the room is still the same, now.

This place is too messy to be enshrined. We have to clean it up — and sell it. There is absolutely no way we can go on living here. Nor any reason to, now that Malcolm is gone.

I looked around. Stuffed animals, stretchy sleepers, and other baby paraphernalia loomed, in piles, around the room. Stacks of congratulatory notes and cards littered the bureau. A case of diapers sat unopened on the floor.

Suddenly a ringing doorbell sent shock waves through me. Who would be calling on us today? My instincts told me to dive under the crib and hide. I should have. Instead, I went dutifully downstairs and opened the door. Standing on the front stoop was a neighbor, with her seven-month-old baby perched on her hip.

"I know you want to be alone, but I just had to come and tell you how sorry I am," she said. "It's just the worst possible thing that could ever happen to anybody."

As she spoke, I thought, "No, she is wrong. The worst possible thing is for her to be standing here in front of me *with a baby in her arms.*" A fat, healthy baby. I couldn't take my eyes off it. All the babies I had looked at in recent months had been pale and sickly, attached to wires and breathing tubes. It was unthinkable for a baby to be strong enough to be outdoors on a fall day, breathing the chilled air. She pushed her infant higher up on her hip and kissed it on the top of its head. Was she flaunting her good fortune in my face or was I losing my mind? How could anyone be so clueless as to bring a baby to visit me at this moment?

"Isn't there anything I can do for you?" she asked. Yes, there was. She could turn around and walk away, but she wasn't about to oblige. Her conversation became a litany of how horrible my situation was. "The worst possible thing has happened to you. You'll never get over it," she said, with a mix of terror and pity in her eyes.

I was speechless.

Then somehow I had let her in and she was looking around the house, with great interest, at the disheveled, broken life inside.

"I really like the color you chose for the kitchen," she said.

Her baby had been squirming; he began to cry out and finally farted. My breasts let down, but I maintained a poker face. I sensed this woman wanted to see some drama, to witness my despair, to have details of my pathetic state of mind to gossip about with the neighbors. She was a voyeur, but she wasn't going to get a tear or even a trembling lip out of me.

It became clear that the baby had soiled its diaper. The smell nauseated me. I told my neighbor I was tired and needed to lie down. She seemed disappointed, as though she had been hoping I would offer her a cup of tea.

"But what are you going to do?" she said, as I coaxed her out of the house.

"I don't have a clue," I said, shutting the door hard and leaning my back against it. The stench from the baby's bowels lingered in the air and made me dry-heave. I retreated to the couch and heard voices outside.

"Molly? Molly?"

I peeked out the window. A group of neighborhood children had assembled in the front yard. They must have seen the car in the driveway earlier and assumed we were home. During my pregnancy, I used to invite these same kids into the fenced back yard. Molly, with her puppyish gallop, would chase them around, nipping at their heels. Sometimes I served the children juice, my mind blooming with anticipation at the thought of the baby growing inside me, the boy who would someday be one of these kids on the block.

Knowing better than to open the door again, I sneaked to the study at the back of the house, lay down on the floor, and covered my ears with a throw pillow from the couch. We had to get out of here for good. I never wanted to set foot in the place again, never wanted to walk on the sidewalks in this town, never wanted to see any of the resident children or their parents. In fact, I decided, we would leave town as soon as Bill got back from the store. The only place I felt I could go to in comfort now was my parents' house in Princeton. This house certainly wasn't home. Their house wasn't either, anymore, but it was better than being here. I would call my parents and tell them we were coming, that night.

I had no idea how much time elapsed before I had the courage to take the pillow off my head. It was quiet outside; the children had gone. I looked at the clock: 2:00 P.M., November 6, 1982. Malcolm had been dead for twenty-three hours. I was counting.

Waiting for UPS

"Where are you, Malcolm?" I whispered, alone in the middle of my parents' living room. "Where have you gone?"

Nothing but hollow silence answered me. The saggy chairs and couches I had grown up with sat there, dumb and unmoved. I lashed back, punching the couch pillows with my fists, my arms enraged at having nothing to cradle. An angry, frightening void was growing inside me in a place where, only months before, Malcolm had ripened.

I became convinced I would feel less empty and confused once I had Malcolm's ashes. The tacky urn would be something tangible to hold, a container carrying at least a fragment of my son — even if it was de-alchemized into ash. Possessing the little box might somehow quell my nerves. Maybe, feeling its palpable weight, I would stop obsessing about where in the universe my son had gone.

The ashes were supposed to arrive by UPS. Such a bizarre delivery. I didn't want to leave my parents' house, for fear of missing the truck and having to face a yellow "attempted delivery" slip in the front door.

*Waiting, I train Molly. We pad the downstairs rooms, working on "heel, sit, stay, and come." Sensing my underlying hysteria, Molly never disobeys me. But she's only seven months old; she gets tired, so I unleash her and walk alone, always taking the same route. I start in the living room, make a **U** through the room we call the sunporch, go down two steps into the dining room, take one lap around the table before pushing through the swinging door into the pantry. As a child, I used to stare at the New Yorker covers my father hung for wallpaper. I would run my hands over the bumpy sink counter he tiled into a colorful mosaic and feel the sting in the air of yesterday's martinis. Now, twenty years later, I stand at the sink rubbing the same tiles and trying to clear hospital images from my mind.*

Next, I walk up the two steps into the kitchen and down the front hall. I loop through Mother's study, pass the front door, and reenter the living room, ready to start my frantic house tour again. From childhood, I know every creaky floorboard, the worn spots on the steps, and the shifting patterns the sunlight makes on the rugs. I stop to stare out the windows at the roof lines of the neighboring houses. These buildings and their surrounding landscapes have appeared in my dreams for more than twenty years. Everything around me is as familiar as the freckles and veins on my forearms and, yet, I feel like a stranger.

I've grown up, moved away, and started a family. I'm not supposed to be back; but here I am — empty, uprooted, homeless.

Molly watched my progress around the house, her head down, bovine, her sad brown eyes tracking my perpetual motion. When I was too frustrated to take another step, I would lie on the floor with her, petting her shiny black shoulders and burying my face in her soft ruff. She smelled like scalp and soil and fresh air. I talked to her in a stream of consciousness. I thanked her for her steadfastness. I couldn't imagine enduring this hell without her companionship, her warm presence. In her quiet way, Molly seemed to understand. Not given to licking, she would rest a sympathetic paw over my arm. As Emily Dickinson said: Dogs are even better than people, because they know, but they do not tell.

Most days Molly and I had the house to ourselves. My parents both worked and Bill was finishing up yet another script, this one promoting, of all things, Alaska. He spent long stretches in the library or in New York working with the production crew.

Like all the women in my family, I had always been a bad napper, but I was getting so little sleep at night that, fearing I might drop off at any time, I parked myself close to the front door so I'd be ready when the UPS truck came. I needed those ashes.

Sleep, when it did come, brought no relief. I dreamt only about Malcolm. In one dream, he was alive but amphibious, living in a brown paper bag. I peeked in at him constantly, worried because there was no water in the bag. His brilliant blue eyes sparkled at me, but I could never see the rest of his body. Somehow he was surviving in there even though it was desert dry. I knew he couldn't last long and I was desperate to help him, but I couldn't.

In another dream, Malcolm was four years old and an avid bike rider. We had moved to a hilly neighborhood. The doctors cautioned us not to let him ride his bike up the hills. Strenuous activity, they explained, might make his heart explode. But all he wanted to do was ride. And I had to tell him no, again and again.

Women of my mother's crowd who had lost babies appeared in my dreams. Mrs. Green, the mother of my friend across the street, had lost three of her five babies. As a child I had known about this tragedy, but hadn't given it much thought. Now Mrs. Green was a regular figure in my dreams.

Dream: Mrs. Green helps me pack for a long journey. I put several T-shirts and pairs of shorts in my suitcase. She takes them out and replaces them with sweaters, long pants, heavy tights, and several pairs of wool gloves.

"I've never seen any of these clothes before," I say. "And I don't want them anyway. I'm going south."

"No, you aren't," she says. "You'll need all these things and more."

Another neighbor, Mrs. Carpenter (whose baby had actually died of Sudden Infant Death Syndrome before that disaster had a name), calls me on the phone to give me a weather report.

"You must be prepared," she says.

I'm frustrated with these women. They don't get it. I'm not going where they say I'm going. There's something ominous and dark about this place they keep mentioning.

"You've never been there before, but you're going now," says Mrs. Green. The sad look on her face scares me. I'm afraid she's going to cry. "I know," she says. "I've been there and you too must go."

Nancy, one of my older sisters, took a few days off from her job in a Pennsylvania bank to come visit me. She and her husband had no children — they didn't want any — but she brought her schnauzer mix, Daisy. Molly and Daisy, the "cousins," got along well, although Daisy, being smaller, had to growl periodically to keep up her pretense to alpha status. Molly tumbled Daisy good-naturedly and chased her around the house, but would periodically look back over her shoulder at me. She seemed to be checking on her sad mistress.

Nancy knew about grief. She and her husband had lost their German shepherd, Zappa, a dog so well-trained you could tell him to "stay," then dangle a sirloin steak in front of his nose. He would drool and whimper, but never budge until given permission. At age ten, Zappa got cancer. For a while, he held his own, but then the disease worsened sharply. They decided to drive him to the Animal Medical Center in New York. On the way, Nancy realized it was a hopeless mission. Zappa was a goner. An attendant met them, took the leash from her, and led him away. At the end of the hall, before turning onto another corridor and out of sight, Zappa stopped and looked dolefully back at his master and mistress, as if to say, "This is it. I just want one last look at you folks." Or maybe he was thinking, "Are you really going to let this happen to me?" For years, the image of that dog, turning back to take one last look at his people, had haunted me.

Now, I had my own image: Malcolm sucking on his pacifier, looking around, looking at me and Bill. I could still feel his grip on my pinkie. Again and again in my mind, I uncurled his fingers from mine and told the doctor he could take him. I felt his soft cheek against my lips. These images seemed indelibly carved on the back side of my eyes, a frieze of grief.

While she was at the house, Nancy and I slept in the double bed in her old room, the one we had shared so often as children. I lay awake all night, listening to her steady, calm breathing, longing for sleep myself but unable to drift off because of the scary scenes that paraded through my head.

I tried to think about sleeping in this bed with Nancy, when we were little girls. We had played a game called "squirrel," where we rounded up our favorite stuffed animals and trinkets and pushed them down to the foot of the bed, between the sheets, the way squirrels store nuts. Then, in the dark, when we were supposed to be sleeping, we would pull out our toys and play with them.

The wind rustled the evergreen trees outside Nancy's windows, a familiar sound from long ago. I tried to distract myself by remembering the other games Nancy and I used to play. But like a news alert flashing across a television screen, the image of Malcolm crying, struggling for air, and all alone in his isolette, returned to overwhelm all the other pictures. How could I have ever left him alone?

I kicked off the covers on my side of the bed and sat up, sweating, guilt-ridden. I had left him again: but this time Malcolm was going to be alone . . . forever.

In the morning, Nancy asked me how I had slept. "Fine," I told her. She and I were close, but a chasm as wide as the Grand Canyon was opening between us. I was ashamed of my obsessive thoughts and raging feelings. They seemed too grotesque to share with anyone. I knew I needed (as my family had always said) to "get hold of myself." How long was this going to drag on?

Having the ashes in hand, that would help.

Finally, the urn arrived. Nancy, Bill, and I stood silently in the kitchen while I unpacked the box. I set the bronze urn with "Malcolm" engraved across one side on the kitchen counter. We looked at the ridiculous thing and cried.

How stupid I had been! Malcolm wasn't in that silly box, that fancy tea tin. What had I been expecting, my son delivered, transformed into a sort of Holy Grail? I didn't even bother to pry open the top. I knew without looking that whatever was inside was of no value to me. It wasn't my child.

Circling

Everyone was home — my mother, my father, and Bill.

I slipped out the front door. The air was damp and raw and foggy. I walked up the driveway all the way to the end and turned left behind the garage. A row of hemlocks and a stone wall separated our property from Mrs. Goodrich's, the wealthy, elderly widow who lived behind us. She had formal gardens and Italian groundskeepers who kept her leaf pile brimming with fresh leaves. I crossed my parents' sodden, grassy backyard. Behind me stood the tall stucco wall and the stile we had climbed, as kids, to get to the top of the wall; from there we would leap, with abandon, into Mrs. Goodrich's huge leaf pile on the other side. Abandon. I knew I'd never feel the joy of it again.

At the side of the house, I opened the gate of the picket fence I had once had my friends help me whitewash, as in *Tom Sawyer.* I walked down the flagstone path, turned, and jogged past the perennial beds. The plants were tied back and dead looking, like bound straw. They leaned heavily toward the ground, dormant for the winter. Down two steps and one more walkway and I was back at the driveway, ready for another lap.

Circling again, I reached the soggy backyard and, from there, could see my parents sitting on the sunporch, framed like Whistler paintings, in long yellow rectangles of light. Their lips were moving. Out here it had grown dark and they couldn't see me. I was all alone. Flannery O'Connor described illness as a place, a room the sick entered, where no one else could follow. Grief worked the same way. No one, not even Bill, could take this journey with me.

I shivered from the cold. What was I doing out here? I called softly for Molly. But why? I knew I had left her inside. I called for Malcolm.

"Where are you, son?" I whispered, feeling a bit like a bad Shakespearean actor delivering a soliloquy on a soupy night.

"I need to find you," I said. I knew the absurdity of such a quest, but I was determined. "Where have you gone?"

Silence.

"Are you in the trees? In the air?"

Silence.

"Why did I ever let you out of my body? You were safe there, beating with my heart, and you knew it. That's why they had to cut you out. You had no intention of coming by yourself. You knew better. Where are you?!"

I listened. Nothing. A raindrop splatted onto a piece of flagstone. Loud, bubbling mud oozed up around the stones as I stepped. The earth had frozen once and thawed, probably for the last time before the deep cold silenced it.

"I'm so thankful we didn't bury you in the earth, Malcolm," I said. "You'd be so cold . . . you'd be freezing."

I reached up to grab a familiar branch of the crabapple tree, one of my favorite childhood climbers. Pain jolted through my breasts like an electric current. I staggered and almost fell. I had forgotten.

"Malcolm?" I whispered.

Every cell in my body seemed to be screaming for my son. I wanted to yell, but didn't dare. Fog and silence enveloped me.

"Carol?" It was my mother's voice, bell-clear but edgy. She was standing at the front door. "Are you out there?"

I wanted to run to the backyard and hide — my new response, it seemed, to every human encounter — but she had seen me.

"What have you been doing out here?" she asked. "And with no coat on!"

"Nothing," I said.

Dutifully responding to her tone, her maternal presence, I walked back in through the door she held open for me.

Church

It was early Sunday morning. Malcolm was eight and a half days dead. I was heading out the door with Molly for a walk in the woods, wondering how I was going to endure the rest of my life. There were no answers today. All I knew was that I needed to be in the woods, close to nature, alone with my dog.

"Would you like to go to church with me this morning?" Mother asked. I told her I'd think about it on my walk.

Molly and I had been spending hours in the secluded forest behind the Institute for Advanced Study, Princeton's "think tank." The only people I saw back there were the resident geniuses, ambling along the paths, hands thrust deep into pockets, their eyes fixed on some point in the space in front of them, their minds worlds away from me, the pale woman with the damp face and the obedient black dog. I felt invisible in the woods, anonymous. Safe.

Invariably, Molly led me off the path, through some ferns to a mossy spot deep in a stand of arching hardwoods, our private sanctuary. There I could lie face down on the spongy earth. Being on my stomach no longer hurt my breasts; my milk, having finally given up, had been reabsorbed into my body. Each day, it seemed, my bust shrank a cup size. But it was no comfort: I was the character from *Madame Bovary* — the daughter of the old fisherman, Guerin — who was always sad. Everyone said she suffered from what they called "a fog in the head." The doctor couldn't help her nor could the priest. During her worst attacks, the customs officer would find her stretched out, face down in the pebbles on the beach, crying. Lost in my own fog, I let the cold moisture seep into my bones, feeling Malcolm's presence all around me. I saw his face in the moss. I heard his short, labored breaths and saw the strain in his nostrils as they flared for air. He was everywhere and yet nowhere, like the Cheshire Cat. And I was convinced I was losing my mind.

I tried to clear my head, think of other things. Mother wanted me to go to church. Why did the idea make my stomach churn? I remembered a recurring nightmare I had suffered when I was eleven. In the dream, I was alone with my oldest sister, Susan, in the house late at night. We were trying to go to sleep in the twin beds in her room. Susan and I had always shared a little relaxation ritual: Lying on our backs, we would each put an arm out to the other, making a bridge across the space between the two beds. With our free hands, we would gently tickle each other's extended arms. When it was time to change arms, we would change beds. This innocent ritual became the ominous, foreboding first act of my nightmare.

At a certain point in the dream, we would become aware of sibilant voices and a faint scratching at the front screen door. In the dream, I always knew we were not alone. There were dangerous men down there, slitting the screen door, breaking into the house. We stopped tickling each other's arms to listen. Susan wasn't scared, but I was petrified.

"Come on," I whispered. "We've got to hide in the attic."

Susan didn't want to move, but I forced her to get up. As we tiptoed out of her room and up the attic stairs, we could hear the men advancing to the second floor. Desperately, I begged her to hide with me far back in the attic, behind some trunks. She followed me, but brushing the whole thing off: "You are being ridiculous," she whispered. We had nothing to fear — because God was on our side.

Below us, someone pushed open the attic door. The landing light flooded the attic stairs, turning them bright white. Susan wanted to move closer, to get a better view.

"You're crazy," I whispered. "Those men are at the bottom of the stairs. They'll see you."

"Don't worry," she said, dismissing me with a big sister's nonchalance and a contemptuous roll of her eyes. "I have God with me."

I grabbed her by the nightgown and begged her not to leave me, but she pulled away and walked quietly to the top of the stairs. I could see her entire form frozen in the beam of light. Two gunshots rang out. I watched her crumble, saw the blood soaking her yellow cotton nightgown, heard her body thump heavily down the stairs. She was dead, and I knew I would be next. I heard the killers' boots coming toward me on the attic stairs. . . .

And that was when I always woke up, clutching my sheets.

By day, I smiled and played with my friends, splashing in the club pool. I looked carefree, like all the other kids, but underneath the sunny facade I was filled with dread. Every evening, as the languid afternoons turned shadowy and darkness descended, my anxiety increased. Soon I would have to go to bed and worry about having my Godforsaken (literally!) serial nightmare. Even on the hottest nights, I could not sleep if the screen door was the only barrier between me and the outside world. I would sneak downstairs after everyone else had gone to bed to close and bolt the big wooden door. In my room, I made sure to lock the windows. Mary McCarthy observed that when she was twelve she pretended to lose her faith, in a ploy for attention, and then realized she had really lost it. Maybe something happened to the spirits of pre-adolescent girls. I felt I had been abandoned by God.

A crow squawked in a branch nearby, probably alerting its kin to the woman lying on the damp earth, her dog at her side. Suddenly, I thought about the Peruvian woman whose four-year-old son had been stationed across from us at Boston Children's Hospital. When he died suddenly, she threw herself down, beat her head against the floor, and shouted again and again, *"Porque Dio? Yo quiero nada!"* The hospital staff had to restrain her with a hypodermic and carry her away on a gurney. I couldn't get the image of the woman flailing on the floor like a freshly caught fish on a pier out of my mind.

I forced myself to get up off the soft and forgiving ground, brushed the leaves off of me, and headed back to the path. Low clouds scurried rapidly across the darker sky. I breathed deeply. In the woods was where I belonged. I'd once seen a bumper sticker that I recorded in my journal: "Earth is my God and nature is its spirit." I had no use for church or my mother's God, but I would go with her to a service. It might make *her* feel better.

We sat toward the front of the University Chapel, the biggest church in town. I had picked it because it was the most impersonal and the most beautiful. The enormous space smelled dank and muddy. Massive columns like an allée of trees met high above us in classic Gothic arches. There were huge stained glass windows. But no amount of beauty or majesty could stop the struggle going on in my mind. Even over deafening organ music, I could still hear Malcolm gurgling in my ears. I looked around, appalled at the contrast between the solid, patriarchal permanence of the chapel walls and the transience of my son's tiny, evanescent body.

The choir marched in. I thought back to my wedding, held among the ornately carved wooden benches in the rambling choir stall of this very chapel. How hopeful Bill and I had been for our future life that day. As we had walked down the long main aisle afterward, tourists sitting in pews wished us congratulations and good luck. We'd had a good marriage, a great marriage, a lucky marriage. We withheld nothing from each other; we didn't compete with each other or, out of insecurity, try to diminish each other. Bill seemed to understand everything about me, the way a woman friend would. In Jungian psychology, one would say Bill had a well-developed feminine side, a good relationship with his anima, his soul. We were a solid couple, but our luck as parents was miserable.

The minister's sermon was about the importance of forgiveness. I couldn't imagine forgiving — not to mention believing in — a God that had taken Malcolm from us after cruelly teasing us with such exquisite false health and hope. Malcolm's death was an inexcusable error.

At the end of the hour, the minister told everyone to greet each other. A tall man's face leaned down toward mine.

"Good morning," he said.

I hung my head and reached for Mother's hand. I couldn't meet his gaze.

"Please get me out of here," I whispered to Mother, as a torrent of tears overflowed my eyes. As far as I was concerned, once past the ritual element, superficial well-wishing and social-hour coffees were what church was all about. And I wasn't about to accept the empty greetings of strangers.

Tea with Mrs. Bennett

I lay on my old bed, in my childhood room, Molly curled up at my feet. Cold sleet blew in sheets across the yard, pummeling the storm windows. The weather was too nasty for walking.

Bill had taken the commuter train into New York. I was supposed to have gone with him for a lunch with my erstwhile boss, but try as I might, I hadn't been able to pull myself together to make the trip. Let's face it — I just wasn't the Jackie Kennedy type, able to preside heroically and regally over public tragedy. All I wanted to do was spend my days walking in the woods. The natural palette of the wintry landscape soothed me — brown leaves, black tree trunks, an occasional burst of green fern or moss, a tangle of eggplant-colored vines . . . and the slate gray sky. Most of the vegetation was dead or dormant, and I felt comfortable in its presence. Being cloistered indoors made me think about the mundane, painful tasks that lay ahead.

We had to go back to Wakefield and deal with the gifts that had arrived for Malcolm. I hadn't even had the heart to open them all yet. What would I do with everything? Every day, the mailman delivered a stack of condolence notes to my parents and to Bill and me. I knew a fresh mound of correspondence would be accumulating under the mail slot in Wakefield, including Malcolm's staggering hospital bills. Each bill was like a stab in the chest, a bleak reminder of another harrowing episode in our baby's short life. How were we ever going to pay all those bills? Plus, we had to finish fixing up the place, sell it, pack it up, and move. We had to find an apartment in Boston. I had to find a new job. Thinking these thoughts made me cold. I pulled another blanket over Molly and me.

In a book I read on grief, the author said the bereaved should never move right away, that there was no way to escape the pain. You couldn't leave it behind—at the last house, in another state, in another country. Grief followed you wherever you went.

But we had no reason to stay. We had no long-standing friends in Rhode Island. We felt no sense of community, had no history in the place. The only good that had come out of our brief stay was Molly.

If I'd written that book, I would have advised people not to move while pregnant, or if they must, to rent, not buy. Then, if your baby dies, you can get out of the deal easier. I'd also tell people to avoid the freelance commuting life, with no built-in professional ties to your new community. I'd say: "Move to a place where you have lots of friends and emotional support . . . in case your baby dies."

But who ever expects their baby to die?

An article on grief warned that a high percentage of couples who lost children broke up after the tragedy. Bereavement was tough on couples who needed to share every experience or who were threatened or angered if their spouse didn't see the experience exactly the way they did. There were examples: A woman accused her husband of being unfeeling because he went to work while she stayed home, unable to think about anything but their dead daughter. It was boorish and insensitive of him to work, she claimed, and she hated him for it. But for him work brought distraction and temporary relief from the pain. She resented his finding any solace when she could find none, and he resented her accusations that he lacked feeling.

I thought about the fisherman's wife who'd had to hide all her feelings from her husband — one tear would send him into a rage. I could scream and cry with Bill, say anything. He wasn't frightened by my grief. I was more scared of it than he was.

In any case, it was decided: We *were* going to move. And I knew we weren't going to split up, even though our responses to Malcolm's death had been, and would continue to be, completely different. I was the one who had carried Malcolm those nine months. I had borne him, fed him, and cared for him constantly. Bill had been involved too, but we both knew he hadn't felt the same bond and that was all right; it was natural. I didn't hold it against him for not feeling the loss as intensely as I did. I was grateful he was able to work. After all, somebody had to pay the bills!

Once we had moved to Boston, I would have to look for work. I sighed. How was I going to do all these things when I barely had the energy to drag myself out of my bed in the morning? Having always been a nervous type, a busy person who feared idleness, I was frightened by my leaden despondency. I had to get up. I had to do something with myself. I rearranged my feet around Molly. She began to pant slowly and hopped down from the bed, curling herself into a ball before settling beside me on the floor. *I had to get a life.* I closed my eyes and longed for a dreamless sleep that wouldn't come.

Mother tapped softly on my door and came in. A neighbor of hers, Mrs. Bennett, whose husband had died recently, wanted to come see me.

"I told her she could come for a cup of tea after lunch."

"You *what?*" I asked. I barely knew this woman, hadn't seen her in years. Had she even come to our wedding? I couldn't remember; Mother had invited dozens of her friends, people I hardly knew. Mrs. Bennett was a frail, Southern lady who had always seemed ancient to me, even though she had a daughter several years younger than I was. Her deceased husband had been a judge. Growing up, I had barely known any of the Bennetts. The daughter, Lisa, had gone to private school in town — or perhaps it had been boarding school somewhere, I couldn't remember. I never saw her and I'd never been in their house. The only member of the family I was acquainted with was their black lab, Tarzan, who used to comb the neighborhood in those days, looking for garbage.

"I would barely recognize the woman," I protested. "Why are you letting her come see me?"

"She insisted," Mother said. "I don't know why."

All morning my stomach tossed at the thought of the impending visit. Of all people in the world, why would a near-stranger like Mrs. Bennett be coming? Aside from my sisters, my parents, and my husband, I wasn't seeing

103

anyone. I hadn't even called any friends in the ten days I'd been at my parents' house. When people called me, Bill handled them. How was I supposed to get through this visit without having a complete meltdown, a grief attack like the one I'd had in church?

Despite the rotten weather, I took Molly for a short walk around the block. We passed Mrs. Bennett's house. What was she doing in there? What was she planning? I almost hoped some kind of minor tragedy would intervene before lunch, that she would slip and sprain an ankle or get an emergency phone call from Lisa and have to leave town immediately.

As the noon hour approached, my dread thickened. I couldn't eat lunch. What if Malcolm started crying in my ear while Mrs. Bennett was sitting beside me on the couch? What if hospital images flooded my brain? What if I started screaming?

The doorbell rang. I heard mother and Mrs. Bennett chatting in high-pitched tones in the front hall. I had changed out of my sweat clothes, my indoor/outdoor outfit, into a skirt and sweater. The waistband rubbed my still-puffy belly, but at least I didn't look like I had just had a baby or was about to deliver. I sat on the bed in my room, furious at myself for not having gone to New York with Bill.

Mother called for me. What could I do? Have a sudden attack of "the vapors" like my grandmother? She'd had one just before my mother's wedding and almost didn't attend. She missed the reception altogether. No, I had to go down. My knees were shaking as I descended. Could Mrs. Bennett tell?

"Hello, dear," she said, tipping her head to one side to get a better look at my lowered eyes. Her face was porcelain-perfect with make-up, her lips bright red. She had recently been to the beauty shop for one of those puffy Princeton-lady hairdos. I could see through her curly frosted hair to her scalp.

"What a pretty skirt," she said.

"Thank you, Mrs. Bennett," I said, shaking her small, lotioned hand. My voice faltered. Oh no! Was I going to collapse, right there in the front hall? But Mrs. Bennett, paying no attention to my crumbling tone, chattered on, like the Mrs. Bennet in *Pride and Prejudice*, about the lovely slipcovers, "Were they new?" and the dreadful weather.

Mother led us onto the sunporch and disappeared to make the tea. I could have killed her for abandoning me. Molly sat at my feet, like a seeing-eye dog.

Silence. Some people thought a momentary silence in a room signaled that an angel was passing by. I was embarrassed by silence — it just represented one more social failing. I hoped Mrs. Bennett believed in angels.

She gazed at me and smiled. Please, I begged silently, don't let her say something sympathetic that makes me lose it in front of her. I looked down again, feeling hot tears in my eyes. I wanted to dash outside and run all the way to the woods.

"Tell me about Molly" she said. "How old is she?"

"She's seven months," I responded, wishing I were holding Malcolm in my arms and she was asking me how old *he* was. My lip trembled. I pushed the thought and the tears away.

Mrs. Bennett nodded and smiled.

"Where did you get her?" she asked. Her penciled eyebrows went up, like French accent marks.

"I saw an ad in the paper," I said, "when we were househunting."

Oh God, I thought. She'd better not ask me about our house. I knew I couldn't talk about that.

She didn't. She asked me what I knew about Molly's family.

I told her about Molly's mother, how the ad in the paper had said she was such a good retriever she could carry an egg in her mouth without breaking it. The words jerked out of my mouth. I felt out of control, but at least I wasn't sobbing.

I remembered her dog, Tarzan, the black lab, and asked her about him. And then I realized, before she could speak, that he must be dead by now. I hoped she wouldn't say something about his being gone. That would definitely set me off.

"Oh, that wanderin' man," she said, with a laugh. "He was always out stirring up trouble. I often said if he'd been a man he'd have made a wicked politician."

Silence. Another angel. Another social gaffe. I couldn't think of anything to say, anything at all!

I crossed my ankles and wished I could disappear through a trap door in the couch, deus ex machina. Mrs. Bennett's eyes were on me; I could feel them.

"Well," she said, sighing, "the weather certainly is wicked, isn't it?"

"Yes, it is," I said, shaking my head.

As though satisfied I had said enough, Mrs. Bennett took over the conversation. She told me about her daughter, a recent trip to Europe or somewhere. I could barely hear her there was such a roar of fear and grief and long-ing in my ears. She complained some more about the weather. Mother appeared with the tea and then left again. Damn! Mrs. Bennett talked about the delicious tea, "so good with lemon." My throat was lumpy, but I was able to keep my mind on what Mrs. Bennett was saying.

We sipped tea. Finally Mother returned for good. The two of them chatted. I thought about people I knew who could discuss scary and upsetting personal matters with-out showing any emotion. How did they do it? I had ab-solutely no social persona and no willpower, none at all.

"Well, I'd best be getting home," Mrs. Bennett said. We all stood up and walked to the front hall. Mother fetched Mrs. Bennett's coat and umbrella from the closet. On her way out the door, Mrs. Bennett turned and grabbed my hand.

"There," she said. "You did it."

And she was gone.

One Roll of Film

In the camera store, I kept my sunglasses on. The woman next to me was holding up a negative and pointing at something in it. Her friend let out a shriek and gave the other woman a playful shove. "I think you look great!" she said. A young man was making some Xerox copies and chattering with a woman behind a desk.

I felt like a freak from a forlorn planet, an alien unac-customed to happy human banter. But I tried to smile as I handed the clerk the receipt for the photos. I watched him thumb through several drawers brimming with envelopes.

"I can't seem to find these," the clerk told me. "How long ago did you bring them in?"

"My husband dropped them off a week ago today," I said. The day Bill brought them in, Malcolm would have turned seven weeks old. Today, he would be eight weeks.

"You've got to find these pictures," I said, my voice rising.

"Look ma'am, everybody's pictures are important. We know that," the clerk said. "Why don't you call back this afternoon and we'll see if we've found them."

"But you don't underst. . . ." I stammered. It was hot in this place. I tried to breathe deeply, to calm down. Even without the pictures, I did have a few things to remember him by: the birth certificate stamped with his footprint, the identifying bracelets he had worn in the hospital, two gauze caps seamed with first aid tape, his death certificate, the ashes. Suddenly, I wished I had thought to snip a lock of his hair. Why hadn't I done that? I looked at the man behind the counter, my chin drooping. What a fool I had been for not taking a piece of Malcolm's hair. I was breathing too fast. Why was I thinking about all this, here in the camera store?

The man's nose squeezed up around his eye glasses, as though he were smelling something unpleasant. Was it me? He thought I was crazy, didn't he? My expression was scaring him.

"Wait! Here they are!" said another clerk, coming in from the back room.

I paid for the pictures and bolted.

No one was home at my parents' house. I sat down on a couch in the sunporch. There was no sun flooding the space, the day being cold, the sky low and dark, the color of weather-beaten cedar shingles. I was sweating, even though the room was cool.

I opened the envelope. The first picture was a shot of Bill, taken in the delivery room. He was wearing green surgical scrubs, his mask dangling around his neck. The proud father was holding up his minutes-old son and beaming at the camera. Next came three shots of Malcolm and me, taken the day after he was born. I was lying back against the hospital pillows, my face tanned and tranquil. Cuddled in my arms, Malcolm looked up at me, his cheeks and lips pink and full. He was holding my pinkie in his balled fist.

Such blissful ignorance — the doctor away on his fishing trip, no one else swift enough to pick up Malcolm's "murmur." Human error had given us three good days together, days that had made no difference (fortunately) in the final outcome. I pitied the parents who had to face not only their awesome grief, but their justified fury at the doctors for having botched treatments and killed their children.

Next came two shots, taken by a nurse, of Bill, Malcolm, and me on the bed. Bill and I were smiling at the camera. Malcolm's eyes were narrow. Breathing had already become difficult for him. Now, I could see the strain in him, but we hadn't noticed it then.

In the next shot, the drama began: Malcolm on the light table at Rhode Island Hospital, a tube in his belly, an IV in his arm, his body strapped down. It was after his first ambulance trip, the ride he had taken without me. That was the night I had sat beside him until dawn in the rocker Patty Romph had found for me. Next came two pictures of Malcolm, swaddled to hide the heart monitor wires. But there was no disguising the silly little Dixie cup the nurses had taped to his head to protect the IV needle going into a vein in his scalp. It looked like a performing monkey's cap.

There were two shots of Malcolm at home. In one he was sleeping, propped up in his crib; in the other he stared wistfully at the camera from the changing table, again with his upper body elevated. When I had taken those shots, I had tried not to project ahead to this moment, the inevitable future time when I would be studying these photos, without him.

The post-open-heart surgery shots were the hardest to look at. We had actually believed Malcolm would be able to share these at "show-and-tell" someday. All those tubes and bandages, all the pain and suffering he had endured. For what? Now I understood why that first ICU nurse had thought we were crazy to be celebrating and snapping photos.

I flipped on — and was back to the first shot again, the one of Bill holding Malcolm up. And so that was all. A single roll of twelve photos had captured the entire life of my child. There would be no shots of the two of us out for a walk with Molly, of Malcolm sitting up in the high chair someone had lent us, of our son learning to crawl or covered with suds in the bathtub. There would be no children's museums, zoos, and parks; no robust toddler, cheeks puffy, blowing out his birthday candles. There would be no first day of school, no lunchbox in hand, no first missing tooth, no track trophies held high. No graduations.

I put the pictures, along with Malcolm's hospital bracelets, birth and death certificates, homemade medical charts, and condolence notes in an empty box. I took the box upstairs to the guest room, where Bill and I were staying, and slid the carton under my twin bed, knowing that for months, maybe even years, I would reach for it — my own Pandora's box.

In Memoriam

It had been almost a month since Malcolm's death, and we were finally having a memorial service. People had said that a public event, with some sort of eulogy, would bring a sense of completion. I didn't know whether it was true or not, never having been to one, but I was desperate to try almost anything for a sense of closure.

Bill and I sat up front in the little side chapel of the same vast University Chapel where we had been married. This space, like the choir loft, was intimate, a narrow seating area with a simple altar surrounded by small, dark, stained glass windows. One towering stone wall was covered with engraved memorials to Princeton graduates. The place smelled of iron and mold.

I felt eyes on my back. Many of our friends, having traveled from New York and Boston, were sitting behind us. Relatives had come from even farther away. I knew that if I looked back and saw who was there, I wouldn't have the courage to face the crowd and say what I had to say. Even without looking, I wasn't at all sure I would get through this event intact. I felt exposed and embarrassed.

But the responsibility was falling on us to make other people feel comfortable, to show them we were okay. That way, they could feel okay. People needed to be able to say about me, "Oh, it's sad, but she's strong, she's coping, she'll do all right." By my example, others would deduce that, if the same unspeakably horrific thing were to happen to them, they too would be able to cope. But I wasn't coping. I wasn't okay.

The minister, who was a friend of my parents and the man who had married us, opened the ceremony with a short invocation. Then Bill went up to the podium and read a tribute he had written, called "Words for Malcolm."

"I wanted to speak about Malcolm because many of you never had the chance to know him. He would have liked this place, this beautiful chapel, because he liked to look at anything unusual. . . . He had a lanky, well-formed body, with big feet that might someday have carried him down a cinder track, like his grandfather."

Bill's voice broke, but he got it back right away. Hearing snuffling and sobs behind me, I forced my ears to stop listening and stared at my lap, studying the pattern of tiny yellow and blue flowers against the navy background of my dress. The stem of a yellow flower connected to the stem of a white one. Between the two, a tiny blue flower sprang up on a curly tendril. Repeat. I traced a long chain of flowers down my thigh and tried to swallow. My throat seemed to be closing off, rebelling against having to utter words. I sucked my cheeks in and tried to create some saliva. My mouth was as sauna dry.

Now what? I thought about the pattern on the wallpaper in my childhood bedroom. I had spent hours studying the four little blue and green shapes at eye level from my pillow. They made an almost-perfect square. Focusing on that little space and then seeing it burst out and repeat itself in every direction, all over my room, always cheered me up. I could look anywhere in the room and find it, that original square of four shapes. Seeing it made me feel like I was a small section of a larger plan, a carefully constructed universe of safe, repeating patterns. But the universe wasn't safe. Babies died. My baby had died. There was no safety to be had in this world and nowhere to hide. I followed a line of connecting flowers back up my other thigh, trying to gain composure. The pattern swirled before my eyes and repeated itself, but following its rhythm brought no peace. I longed to be anywhere but where I was.

"There's another way we choose to look at Malcolm's coming and going," Bill went on, "not merely as a loss, a baby lost forever, but as a complete life, lived as fully as possible. He was a little man who was born, lived, fought, suffered, and died. And what more do any of us experience but an elaboration of this basic pattern?"

Blue, yellow, white stems. Repeat.

Bill was beside me again. It was my turn to speak. As I walked up front, I could feel that all those years of being a performer — of singing, talking, and dancing in front of crowds — were going to pay off. I had been a pro, and that familiar performance strength began to course through me again, making my blood fiery, but steely and tough. I turned, faced the crowd, and spoke. In an unwavering voice, I thanked everyone for coming and for all their support over the last months. I invited everyone back to my parents' house after the service. I recited a short, awful poem I had written about Malcolm (it was full of clichés and lies) and then closed my remarks with a quote from Hamlet, one that a friend of my mother's had sent us: "Good night sweet prince," I said, my voice ringing loudly

113

through the space, "And flights of angels sing thee to thy rest."

My only desire was that Malcolm had heard Shakespeare's beautiful words.

Afterward, people came to my parents' house for food and drink. Bill and I were upbeat. We were reciting our lines: "We had the best doctors, the most wonderful nurses, and the best care. They did everything possible for him. We were lucky, really."

One good friend, whom I had known since I was twelve and he was a college student at Princeton, took my hand and shook his head. "Say what you will," he mumbled. "It's just so incredibly sad." His lips trembled and, with his index finger, he wiped tears from his cheeks. I put my free hand on his arm and said something lame about Malcolm's valiant struggle.

I couldn't let my feelings show. In fact, I hadn't felt anything at all. I had been numb all day. I had retreated into a blank state of shock, feeling the way I had just after Malcolm died. It was the only way I could survive the onslaught of sympathetic people. The idea that folks could, and would have, supported me in my grief didn't occur to me. At the time, I believed that feelings were one's private business and best kept under wraps in public.

After everyone left, Bill and I complimented ourselves on our behavior, not knowing yet that there could be no real closure without the expression of real feelings. We had made the service easy for everybody and that was what was important. It would have been in bad taste to do otherwise.

"Bill and Carol sound so philosophical," my mother's friend Eleanor told her. "But it's early still. They're only just beginning to realize what has happened to them."

Moving

Two good friends, Sebastian and Katryna, came up from New York to help us get the house ready to put on the market. Sebastian was a voluble Englishman, handsome, with a skinny yet powerful build. He worked as an academic textbook salesman, but was also a poet and a raconteur. While the two men hammered and painted and lugged heavy cast-iron radiators, Sebastian told stories and engaged Bill in lively discussions about literature. (Men always seem to be able to distract themselves better than women.)

Katryna and I packed up the entire house, starting with Malcolm's room. Most of the time I just sat and watched her hands working. She folded each baby item; swept off any flecks of lint with her long, graceful fingers; and gently added it to one of her colorful piles of baby things. One item was a tiny music box pillow that I had wound up and left in Malcolm's isolette whenever I'd had to leave him in the hospitals. Embroidered with a picture of Peter Rabbit, it played, "Here comes Peter Cottontail, hopping down the bunny trail." I had hoped that the tune provided solace in my absence.

My mother's friend, the woman who had originally introduced us to Wakefield, gave Malcolm the pillow. Back when I was pregnant, she had thrown a baby shower for me. We hadn't met many people in town yet, but she managed to put together a group of women, some who were neighbors of mine, others the daughters of her summer beach-club friends.

I thought back to that day, September 13. All the guests had arrived except for Janice, one of my neighbors, who was also pregnant and due six weeks after me. For an hour, we waited to open presents and eat cake. I called Janice's number, but no one answered. She and I had spent a fair amount of time together over the summer, talking about babies and work and houses. I couldn't imagine what had happened to her.

One guest speculated that Janice had gone into labor and that was why she hadn't come. Another woman volunteered that it was bad luck if one of your guests went into labor and couldn't make it to your baby shower.

We all laughed. "Oh, that's just an old wives tale," someone said. "There's not an ounce of truth to it."

Finally, we went on to the cake and baby presents, without Janice. She never arrived or called.

That night, her husband phoned me from the Intensive Care Unit of a women's hospital in Providence. While I was making small talk with my new acquaintances at the shower, Janice had indeed been delivering a premature baby boy, whose lungs were underdeveloped. The doctors also suspected the baby had spinal meningitis. At the time, I couldn't imagine enduring anything so terrible as what she must have gone through. But now, Janice and her baby were home — and everything was fine.

Katryna and I packed things into boxes, which she labeled. She drove our car to return the borrowed clothes to the women who had so kindly lent us hand-me-downs. I ducked down in the passenger seat, too vulnerable to let myself be seen, while Katryna introduced herself to the women, thanked them, and gave back the boxes of unused stuff.

Katryna understood. The two of us had a long history together and were best friends. We had danced in the same companies in Boston and spent long hours in rehearsals and cafes, talking about everything. Both of us were the youngest of all-girl families and both had melancholic, rebellious streaks coupled with Yankee pride that kept us from showing our feelings, except to our closest friends — and sometimes, like now, not even to them. She was now a collage artist in New York and stepmother to Sebastian's two young boys from a previous marriage.

"Do you want me to take the crib and changing table apart?" she asked softly. "Or should I leave them intact?"

"You may as well take them apart, if you don't mind," I said. I felt sorry for her, being there with me. We were both relieved to finish with Malcolm's room and move on to less charged spaces in the house.

After a day's work, the four of us drank a lot of scotch and ate a supper prepared by Katryna.

Every day bills arrived for Malcolm's ordeal — ER expenses, ambulance rides, doctors fees, medications, and hospital stays. The cost of everything was staggering, thousands of dollars more than our medical insurance plan would cover. Bill took time out from working around the house to call the insurance company, the doctors' offices, the hospitals. Trying to figure out the bills took hours. We began to dread the thud of each day's mail coming through the slot. Every piece of medical correspondence made Bill furious, reminding him all over again of Malcolm's pain and suffering, my loss, his own loss.

"Haven't we gone through enough?" he asked. "Now we have to *pay* for everybody's failure?"

One day a letter arrived from a social worker at Rhode Island Hospital. She informed us that we qualified for a special foundation grant that would pay for all of Malcolm's medical expenses over and above what our insurance company covered. This was a program set up by a wealthy Rhode Island couple whose child had undergone expensive cardiac surgery in Massachusetts. They wanted to help others in the same situation. So, whenever a bill came in, all we had to do was forward it to the social worker.

We couldn't believe our good fortune. We stopped bothering to open the envelopes; we just sent them along. Maybe our moving to Rhode Island, the only state in the country with such a program, hadn't been such a random and foolish act after all.

Finally, the house was packed, fixed up, and ready to sell. Sebastian and Katryna headed back to New York. A friend had found us an apartment in Arlington, a suburb outside Boston. He had warned the landlady that we had a dog, but she said that was fine — she loved dogs. We took the place sight unseen.

The movers arrived on a bitter cold morning. The worst of the winter storms had hit farther inland, leaving our roads and sidewalks clear, but the cold was so palpable we could almost see it.

Moving day marked the two-month anniversary of Malcolm's death. I knew one of the movers was going to ask.

"There's all this baby stuff," said Chris, a smiley guy with bulging biceps and long hair pulled back in a leather string. "Where's the baby?"

"The baby died," I said. For days, I had rehearsed my response in the mirror until I could deliver it without shedding a tear. "The baby died." "The baby died."

No one asked any more questions.

I busied myself indoors while Bill and the movers hauled boxes and furniture out to the truck. I didn't want to see any of our neighbors. What were they thinking about our moving out so soon?

That question was immediately followed by another: Why had I paid so much attention, my entire life, to what I suspected other people were thinking about me and my decisions — the neighbors, the movers, the workmen? I had no answers . . . for anything.

Cowering in the back study, I remembered that writer John Cheever had dressed in a suit and tie and gotten on the elevator each morning with his apartment building neighbors, who were on their way to work. When the others got off on the ground floor, Cheever stayed and rode down to the basement, where he changed into grungy clothes and sat down at his typewriter to write fiction all day in a storage room. At five o'clock, he changed back into his proper corporate suit and rode the elevator back up to his apartment, along with the other nine-to-fivers, the people with "real" jobs. How absurd to care so much what other people thought. But I was just as bad.

Finally, we were ready to depart. Just before we left, our furnace shuddered, shaking the whole house, and then shut off. We couldn't get it to fire up again. It seemed like yet another ironic twist of fate: Now it was the heart of the *house* that had given up and refused to beat anymore. A chill began to fill the rooms. I closed the front door, knowing I never wanted to set foot in that house again.

Light was fading from the sky as we pulled out of the driveway. Bill and I followed the moving truck up the highway toward Boston — the route we had traveled so many times to get to Malcolm. I never wanted to drive these roads again, either. Coming up behind a pokey driver, I had to brake suddenly. I glanced in the rear view mirror to make sure the car behind us was slowing down and saw a brilliant orange and red wintry sunset, like the one I had seen the night Malcolm died.

"He's out there somewhere," I said.

"Yes, he is," Bill said. He reached over and massaged my tense shoulder. Both of us had aching backs and necks. Moving does that to you.

Even though we were driving north and east, away from the fiery western light, I knew I wasn't leaving Malcolm behind. And I knew I was driving into darkness.

On the Edge

In the bleak mid-winter,
Frosty wind made moan.
Earth stood hard as iron,
Water like a stone.

Christina Rossetti, *In the Bleak Mid-Winter*

Willow Court

Weeping willow... the tree of memory and mourning.

The old farmhouse we moved into sat squarely at the end of a cul-de-sac called Willow Court. It was a tiny road, directly off Arlington's broad Massachusetts Avenue, with a row of dingy asbestos-shingled houses on one side and a sizable stone Baptist church on the other. Directly across the avenue sat a huge Foodmaster supermarket.

We had rented the second and third floors of half the farmhouse. Our landlady lived downstairs. The entrance to our apartment was up an outside staircase and off a

121

rickety, enclosed second-story porch that sloped precipitously toward the rear of the house. Looking out the back windows, I noticed that the house was perched on the upper edge of a steep embankment. Down below, a brightly lit asphalt parking lot highlighted the old tires and paper trash that littered the treacherous slope of the embankment. Out the front windows, the neon letters "FOODMASTER" glowed red from far across the avenue.

A small dirt yard at the side of the house opened onto the parking lot for the church next door. Except for a towering oak in the corner of our yard, it was a barren landscape. Fitting, I decided.

Inside, a large living room rambled into an old-fashioned kitchen and bath and down a hall toward the rear, where there was a tiny extra room. Up a steep staircase were two garret bedrooms, cramped under the eaves. The more quiet room in the back would have been Malcolm's, I told myself, when we first saw the upstairs. I couldn't stop thoughts like those from jumping into my mind. Now, Bill would use it as an office. The place gave off a dusty odor, like old books; the walls were dirty, the plumbing noisy. What a contrast between these dingy digs and the freshly made-over house we had just left. This move seemed like a giant step backward.

The movers wanted to know where to put everything. Thank goodness Katryna had insisted we label all the boxes "kitchen," "books," "baby," etc. I gazed at the cartons as they came in and realized I had no memory of what was inside them. My memory of the sounds and sights of the ICU was perfectly distinct — as were my conversations with doctors, nurses, and other parents. But more recent events eluded me.

How different I had felt when we moved to Wakefield eight months earlier. With Malcolm swimming happily inside me, I had busily arranged and rearranged furniture and unpacked boxes as fast as they came through the door. Now I didn't want to touch, or do, anything.

The movers left. We doused our faces with cold water because there wasn't any hot. Bill knocked on the landlady's door to tell her the gas hadn't been turned on, but she didn't answer. We lay down on a mattress on the floor in one of the bedrooms. I had found a box marked "blankets," but none marked "sheets."

Moving was hard on Molly too. In Wakefield, she had her favorite spots. Now she circled around the room and whimpered, not knowing where she was supposed to sleep. "Come here," I called to her, and she lay down beside me on the mattress.

Within a few minutes, Bill was asleep. Molly took a few deep breaths and seemed to be drifting off too. Truck traffic from the busy avenue rattled the windows. The street lights cast a glaring green hue across the floor of the room. My nose tickled from breathing dust. I could feel the mattress sloping toward that gaping hole out back.

Even though my eyes burned from exhaustion, I couldn't sleep. I wanted to cry, but, now that I had privacy, I felt as dry as a crisp pile of raked autumn leaves.

Then I heard it—Malcolm breathing gently in my ear. The breaths grew noisier, coming in short gasps. He was grunting. It was heart failure. His face pushed against mine, growing bigger and bigger with each grunt. His body shook and he began to cry.

I sat up and looked around the unfamiliar room. I called for him. He must be sleeping in the back bedroom,

I thought. And then it hit me: He wasn't there. He wasn't anywhere. My eyes met Molly's. She was lying at the foot of the mattress, staring at me with her wrinkled forehead and sad expression.

I went downstairs and saw all the boxes. And then I remembered everything. I cleared a pile of stuff off the couch and sat down, determined to remain upright and awake. I didn't know if I'd been dreaming or had actually been visited by Malcolm's spirit. Whatever had happened, I didn't want to experience it again.

Over the past two months, I had often woken up feeling worse than when I'd gone to bed. The only solution was to avoid sleep altogether. From the couch, I looked out at the bright FOODMASTER sign across Mass Avenue. Something warm appeared in my lap; it was Molly's head. "Come on up, girl," I said. Eagerly, she hopped up and nestled beside me. That's what I'd always loved about dogs; they're always ready.

The unfamiliar pale green light given off from the street lamp was bright enough to write and read by. My purse was on the couch. I fumbled inside it, finding my journal, and read.

Dream: I'm at a party at the Green's house. Mrs. Green approaches me, arms outstretched for a hug, tears in her eyes. I say, "Oh no, there's been a mistake. You're wrong. Malcolm is okay. We're only moving, that's all. He's alive and well."

I explain to her that we're leaving a house full of funereal equipment — massive sideboards, with dead people laid out on top, covered by white sheets. Gaudy candelabra, with grotesque gargoyles leering from the bases, light up the rooms. Linoleum tiles from the ceiling have dropped onto the floor.

I'm terrified that the house won't sell. A woman comes to look at it. I meet her at the door, hoping I can convince her to buy the place without showing her the horrors inside. "Why are you selling?" she asks. I tell her we are moving because our son, who was born in September, died in November. I tell her not to worry; he didn't have a contagious disease. The woman looks at my face and starts screaming. I know I will never sell the house once people hear the truth about why we are selling.

Our landlady had invited us down for a hot breakfast and said we could wash up down there.

"You go," I told Bill. "I'd rather stay up here."

"She said you could bring Molly," Bill said, obviously hoping that would convince me. "Come on. You're going to have to meet her eventually."

Reluctantly, I went, leaving Molly to nap in the living room. She had experienced enough disruption in the last twenty-four hours. So had I. I stalled on the enclosed porch to watch the activity in the church parking lot. It was a day-care center. Cars pulled up and people got out, carrying bundled babies. Parents held the mittened hands of older children and inched their way across the blacktop, the frigid January wind making them clutch themselves with their free hands. One after another these folks, children in tow, filed into the back door of the church. Several rooms inside were lit up. One set of windows had a snowflake-patterned paper chain draped across the mullions. I watched as the parents hurried back to their cars and drove off.

Marty, our landlady, was a tall woman with short, frosted hair and bright blue eyes. "Welcome to Willow Court," she said, putting an arm around me and ushering me in from the cold. She was preparing a huge breakfast of hot cereal, eggs, bagels, juice, and coffee.

I smiled, but felt wild and shaky. Clenching my jaw, I looked around her apartment and tried to force my heart to beat more slowly. Indian-print bedspreads covered sofas, books were crammed onto overstuffed shelves, framed mandalas hung on the walls. Her place reminded me of a comfy communal pad out of the 1960s. It felt like a true home, so unlike our stark digs upstairs.

I had the feeling someone must have already told Marty about our situation. She was so cheerful and seemed oblivious of my dark, icy mood. She told us that she managed a bookstore; she and Bill then chatted about books. I sat and stared at the bowl of oatmeal Marty had set in front of me. My mind was far away. I was thinking about a healthy little girl named Jessica, who always had to accompany her mother to the hospital to visit her older brother, Sam. I used to watch her, sitting on the floor beside her brother's hospital bed, furiously wrapping and unwrapping her doll in a crib-sized hospital blanket. I could almost see her pent-up energy, an aura of frustration surrounding her small frame. Occasionally, she cast a worried glance in her brother's direction. How much of her short life had been spent crouching beside hospital beds? How was the constant trauma affecting her psyche? She needed to be at a day-care center or a playground. She needed to be running free.

Moments from the past — like watching Jessica play — seemed so much more real than this moment at Marty's table. What was happening to me? Two months had passed since Malcolm's death. I was getting worse, not better, with the passage of time. I had no control over my thoughts or my emotions anymore.

Before we had left Wakefield, I thought nothing would be harder than packing up the house. But as I sat in Marty's cozy apartment, nothing seemed more daunting than going back upstairs and *unpacking*. The grief book had been right: Moving was a terrible mistake. But so was staying put. There was nowhere on Earth I wanted to be.

Still ignoring my boorish silence, Marty told me about a woodsy park where I could run Molly off-leash. She gave me her phone number at work and told me to call her if I needed anything.

On our way out I managed to whisper a meager "Thank you."

I sat on the couch like a stiff, staring at the stacks of boxes. How long would we live here? Where would we go next? When would my bleak mood shift?

In need of support, a grieving person can turn to community (I had none), to God (again, none), and to family (besides Bill, I had my parents—but they were far away). If only I had a job or at least a clear career track (again, zip). I had quit dancing, quit massage, left my job as a community organizer. I had quit a part-time job at the bookstore in Los Angeles, stopped walking people's dogs in New York. I was trying to write children's books and working on a few essays, but nothing had even seen the light of day. I ghost-wrote business scripts for Bill. That was it. I wasn't even a mother anymore.

Self-pity overwhelmed me. I continued to sit, comatose. Molly came into the room, sat beside me momentarily, then trotted back into the hall and whimpered. She had to go out! Bill had taken her to our little wasteland of a yard at dawn, but she hadn't been walked since. He wouldn't be home for hours. My watch told me it was one o'clock in the afternoon. I couldn't believe I had slumped on the couch all that time. There was so much to do around the apartment. But I couldn't face unpacking, and Molly needed a walk.

Despite the gloomy day, I donned sunglasses, knowing my eyes were puffy and red. We found the park Marty had told me about. There were trails through the bone-chilling wooded hills and down below, a frozen pond with a path around it. Beyond the pond was a huge flat field, now snow covered, for picnics and games. The winter landscape reminded me of a Breugel painting, minus the frolicking crowds. Luckily for me, the place was deserted.

We stomped over all the trails, then looped around the black-iced pond. A book on grief suggested reciting a poem or a prayer for relief. I tried to comfort myself by whispering the Twenty-third Psalm: "He leadeth me beside the still waters. He restoreth my soul. . . . Yea, though I walk through the valley of the shadow of death . . ."

The psalm wasn't doing anything for me, so I tried Emily Dickinson:

> There's a certain slant of light
> Winter Afternoons —
> That oppresses like the Heft of Cathedral Tunes.

Molly dashed through the woods, tail wagging, nose to the ground. She trailed squirrels and chased the sticks I threw. Her joie de vivre lifted my spirits. Dogs had always been my soul mates. My childhood mutt, Rebel, used to run beside me when I rode my bike. We would head for the park near my house and I would lie in the grass with her and stare up at the cloud formations, feeling lonely but not alone. Later, when I was a high school student spending time in downtown Princeton with my hippie friends, I would often see Reb trotting up Nassau Street, the main road through town, with her long tongue hanging out. I'd call her over to the grassy lawn where we were all sitting and she and I would have a goofy reunion. If I had any money, I would buy her a hamburger and we would walk home together. She was better company than most of my friends.

Reb had been an inner-city stray, picked up on the streets of Harlem. Skinny and sickly, she had been taken to the Animal Medical Center, where my father was an administrator, to be fattened up before being used for an experiment in open-heart surgery. But one of the doctors fell in love with Reb and couldn't bring himself to operate on her—dogs never survived the procedure. Thinking she was a full-bred boxer, he clipped her tail and ears and took her home to his apartment. The doorman greeted him with a shake of the head. No dogs allowed.

So my father brought her home. I was eight, the perfect age to acquire a dog. It was love at first sight. I walked her and groomed her and hugged her. My mother and I took her to dog school and she won a trophy for fourth place (the highest they would allow a mutt to place). Reb would sit patiently at the base of a tree, waiting for me to finish scrambling to the top. She slept with me in my bed. I told her all my problems. If I could never have another baby, at least there were plenty of dogs in the world.

Molly bounded up to me and deposited a stick at my feet. I tossed it into a dense thicket and she dashed after it. How ironic, I thought. My childhood dog had been spared open-heart surgery, the very procedure that had killed my son.

Genes

One thing I knew for sure: Terrified though I was about having another child, I desperately wanted to get pregnant again. And Bill wanted another baby too, as soon as possible.

The doctors at Children's Hospital had recommended we first see a genetic counselor and wait for her verdict, so Bill had made us an appointment. Now, waiting in the counselor's foyer, I felt like I was on my way to see a fortune teller. "Analyze my genes, woman, and tell me if I'll ever be able to have a healthy child." She had already reviewed both my and Bill's medical histories, as well as all the records on Malcolm's heart defect. She would tell us if she thought Malcolm's condition was likely to be repeated in another baby.

The dreaded appointment only took about ten minutes. Our counselor, a middle-aged woman with hair that stood out from her head like a big, blond helmet, led us into her office and motioned for us to sit in the two chairs facing her desk. She sat down and, without introductions or small talk, started explaining her findings.

She suspected that the flu I caught right after I got pregnant was the most likely culprit.

"A coxsackievirus B could have caused the defect," she told us. "But so could any number of environmental factors." These, unfortunately, we'd never be able to pinpoint. But the good news was that she didn't think there was a genetic problem.

The counselor explained that no one would ever know, for sure, why Malcolm was born with such a rare heart defect—it occurred in one in a million babies. But the chances of something similar happening in another pregnancy were minuscule, even negligible. Her recommendations were to find a good OB-GYN and get me checked out before trying for another baby. She suggested I avoid getting pregnant during flu season, if possible, and stay away from cats because they carried a disease in their stools.

Good, we wouldn't have to be subjected to all sorts of genetic testing. My worst fear—that there would be something terribly wrong with our chromosomes, that we wouldn't be capable of having healthy children—had been allayed.

But she warned us that the rate of miscarriage was extremely high among people who had suffered a trauma like ours and that getting pregnant often took couples in our situation nine to twelve months.

I barely heard any of her cautionary notes. We could have another baby! I only had to get to a good doctor, wait to have a menstrual period, and then start trying! I might actually hold my own baby in my arms—soon.

Odious Comparisons

For the first time since Malcolm's death, I felt exhilarated. I decided to turn the little room behind the kitchen into my writing room. I unpacked books, dusted, mopped, and threw open the rear window to air the place out — ten bleak degrees be damned! It was a perfect little nook to write in. I would keep my journal, work on the children's stories I had started in New York, and tackle the corporate writing assignments I was now determined to get.

But that night I couldn't sleep. Earlier in the day a friend had left a message, letting us know his wife had delivered a baby and that everything was all right. It was her second "all right" baby.

One phone message, and my enthusiasm for life and work was suddenly dashed. All our friends — at least those who could conceive — had had babies. I thought of another woman I knew. She had two babies, work she loved, a wonderful house in town, *and* a place in the country.

What did I have? Nothing. A thought kept nagging at me, like a hungry mosquito. At that very moment, while I lay tossing in my bed, people everywhere were checking on their sleeping children and counting their lucky stars that they weren't me. There was a George Eliot quote I had recorded in my journal: "There is no private life which is not determined by a wider public life."

I seemed to be spending hours comparing myself to the other women I knew. So-and-so was twenty-eight and had one newborn baby. I was already two years behind her. The friend whose husband had called was only twenty-seven and already she had two children. It was as though I were doing some sort of bizarre statistical study of childbearing women and plunking myself down on the phantom chart — always behind the eight ball — or playing a game of Monopoly, acquiring a small cache of hope and possibilities, only to lose it all and have to start all over again, with one swift roll of the dice.

Every day I saw women who were blessed with children — at the Foodmaster, the public library, the post office, and, of course, every time I looked out my window at the church day-care center. It seemed to me that everybody I knew was luckier than I was. No one was plagued by the hospital traumas, the career confusion, and the uprooting I had experienced. Maybe what I needed was a demanding commitment, something steady to force me out of bed, a regular job where I had to dress decently and could bury my pain under mountains of work, my vulnerability under make-up and nylons.

Who had I been trying to kid, when I'd left the genetic counselor's office maniacally happy at the prospect of having another baby? Another baby wouldn't ease my angst. Children weren't replaceable, like venetian blinds or down quilts. Malcolm was gone — forever. My life would never be the same again. I felt stony, impenetrable, hopeless.

There wasn't a sound in the apartment, except for Molly's steady breathing. As I lay there, motionless, my face tight and drawn, my heart covetous, I thought about Malcolm's brief and miserable life. He never even had a chance to pet a dog and here I was wasting my time consumed with jealousy of other people's lives instead of valuing my own. How dare I be so selfish?

A concept began to materialize in my mind: Maybe it was true that my life would never be the same again, that the worst thing *had* happened to me. But the thought of spending the rest of it in a state of terminal envy seemed almost as needless a tragedy as to have lost Malcolm in the first place.

"In the final analysis," Harold Kushner wrote, in *When Bad Things Happen to Good People*, "the question is not why bad things happen to good people, but how we respond when such things happen."

My life was mine, mine alone. No one else would ever experience what I was feeling, not even Bill—and that was all right. I was a separate person, a unique individual. For the first time in my life, I was beginning to feel a rich sense of self. Something inside me was beginning to shift. Who cared what everybody else was doing? Other people's business, other women's babies, couldn't be the central cog of *my* life. Nor could my consciousness be governed by what other people thought of my life. Period. This was a tough concept for a competitive person like me, the idea that I didn't have to compare myself to anybody. So what if I didn't have a clearly defined career path at the moment? Who said I had to have one? Who was making the rules? So what if everybody felt sorry for me? That was their business. My business was to lead my own life. I owed that much—and more—to Malcolm. At least I was alive and healthy.

I was tired of judging my life as though I were someone else, someone looking in at me from the outside, a person who seemed at times to have someone else's standards and values, not mine. I had always judged everything in other people's terms: What would she think? How did I look? What did he think of what I said? My goal should be to treasure my life for what it was, no matter how pitiful or painful I thought it seemed to others.

Now, for the first time in my life, the voice of that judgment—the nasty critic/censor, who always knocked on my head, pointed at other people, and whispered critical comments in my ear—was silent. I felt centered, strong.

"Losing a child is by no means a good experience," I had read in a pamphlet somewhere, "but it *is* a deep experience."

I leafed through my journal until I found the quote I was looking for, from the Bhagavad Gita:

Lift up the self by the Self
And don't let the self droop down,
For the Self is the self's only friend
And the self is the Self's only foe.

I put in a call to a friend of a friend, who I'd heard had found a good OB-GYN group. Sure, she had a healthy baby and my baby was dead, but that didn't mean I couldn't talk to her. Don't get mired in comparisons, I told myself. Just call. I had business to attend to and she might be able to help me.

And my voice didn't even quaver on the phone. I simply asked her for the number, called the doctors' office—a group called Urban Woman and Child, in Jamaica Plain—and made an appointment. I did stumble on my words when the receptionist wanted to know if I had any children. Those questions were always tough, but I got through it. Then I called a man who was the sales and marketing director for one of the production companies where Bill freelanced and made an appointment to talk with him.

Hearing car tires spinning outside, I bundled up and went outside with Molly. I helped three people push their cars out of snow banks. I felt like I was a member of the human race again. When we went back upstairs, I sat down in my little office. I was going to work, finally, on my own writing.

Complications

I heard something fall in the living room and the sound of Molly's paws scraping across the wooden floor. I got up from my writing desk to check on her. She was frantically tearing up a newspaper she had knocked off the table.

"Molly!" I shouted. "Stop that!"

She paid no attention to me. Something was odd about this. My impeccably trained dog rushed to the stairs and started tearing at loose strings of carpet fabric. Furiously, she nipped and licked the walls.

In a panic, I dragged her outside to the icy yard. She lurched at the snow, fitfully gulping at it and sneezing. She began to shake all over and her belly was swelling up, like a shiny black balloon. With dawning horror, I decided she must have eaten poison on our walk.

It was after five, but I reached the vet on the phone.

"Bring her in immediately," he said.

As I was loading her into the car, Bill came walking down Willow Court, home early.

"Just get in the car" I yelled from behind the wheel. "Something's wrong with Molly."

He jumped in on the passenger side and took Molly onto his lap. Luckily, I had shoveled earlier and we were able to make our way smoothly through the foot or so of recent snow.

The vet stood Molly up on the exam table. He held her head steady and looked into her eyes. She was gulping air, frantic with fear.

"I'm going to have to knock her out right away," he said, after feeling the pulses in her hind legs. He would x-ray her stomach, he explained, and try to depress the air in it. He suspected she was having an attack of gastric dilatation, a deadly veterinary emergency condition, commonly called "bloat."

"Don't be alarmed," he added, injecting her with anesthetic. "When this hits her, she'll slump suddenly."

She did, crumbling onto the table like an imploding building. He carried her limp body to a back operating room.

Bill and I returned to the waiting area out front and sat on a couch. No one else was in the room. We heard noises drifting down the hallway, the familiar sounds of sliding metal x-ray trays. Here we were again waiting for medical news.

After what seemed an interminable wait, the vet returned. Molly was okay, for now. It was bloat, as he had thought: Her pyloric valve, which leads out of the stomach, spasmed shut, preventing air from leaving the gut. Immediately, her stomach began to blow up and she became frantic, her instinct driving her to graze desperately. He hadn't been able to find any pulses in her hind legs, which indicated that the blood supply had been cut off. If unchecked, the condition could have caused her stomach to flip over in the abdominal cavity, cutting off all blood to the gut. Acute gangrene could have set in and killed her. It can happen to a dog within an hour. Her stomach had been enormous, he said.

"She has a fifty percent chance of a repeat incident," he said. "And if she suffers another episode, her survival chances are fifty-fifty. You'll have to watch her carefully."

Bill carried our drugged, wasted dog to the car. At home, I settled her on the couch and watched her eyeballs wander in their sockets. We both sat with her, listening to make sure her breathing was even. The image of our Molly slumping, deathlike, onto the vet's shiny table pulsed repeatedly through my head.

All my muscles ached from pushing cars out of the snow and lugging Molly up and down the stairs. I needed a hot shower. I let the water pour over my sore body and raised my tight face toward the showerhead. Gingerly, I patted soap onto my tender cesarean incision.

And then I felt it: a distinct lump on my left side, under the stitches.

I called for Bill. He felt the spot and wondered if it was in the same place where Molly had jumped up and pawed me the day I checked out of the Wakefield hospital.

That night, I dreamt I had abdominal cancer, a huge growth the size of Molly's blown-up belly, under my ribs. I had to call my mother and tell her. She fainted at the other end of the line, and I could see her, unconscious on the floor, the phone receiver dangling in midair. I woke up sweating and terrified.

In the morning, I canceled my appointment with the marketing director and called Urban Woman and Child. I needed to come in sooner, I explained shakily to the receptionist. "I have a lump."

She found me an earlier appointment, two days away. Forty-eight hours. The wait seemed an eternity for a hysterical hypochondriac like me, but I would just have to tough it out. I got off the phone and felt for the lump again. Yes, it was still there.

All my life, whenever I discovered something irregular about my body, I would check it obsessively. Once, while riding a train on my way to a modern-dance festival, I had noticed a soft, fleshy lump just above my coccyx. In an instant my entire world view shifted. One second, I had been excited and hopeful about the upcoming summer; in the next, I was filled with dread and a sense of doom. I made repeated trips to the toilet to feel the area, my face pale, knees weak.

Whenever I went into one of these "blindered states," as I called them, I couldn't concentrate on anything except my obsession; happy life events only increased the cruel irony of my circumstances. I was, after all, at death's door, alienated from everyone around me by my secret infirmity.

That particular time, I acted sensibly and told my roommate about my concern. She felt the spot.

"I think I have a lump there too," she said. "I think everybody does."

I felt her back and, sure enough, she had an identical bulge. It was ordinary human anatomy.

But this new lump was different: It was rock-hard, the size of a golf ball, and growing. Nobody else had one of these. The receptionist had told me to apply heat to the area, so I stripped down to take another shower, and on a whim, stepped on the scale. I had lost five pounds — in one week! Was I wasting away? Surely another symptom of imminent death. I got in the shower and pressed a hot washcloth onto the bump. Anxiously, I examined my breasts to make sure *they* were all right and found a pea-sized lump near my right nipple.

I jumped out of the shower and called the OB-GYN office again.

"You're not going to believe this," I said, "but I've got a lump in my breast, too."

"Try not to worry," Suzanne, the nurse practitioner told me. "We'll get you all squared away when you come in."

I hung up and decided she was probably telling the other people in the office: "We've got a real 'case' on our hands with this Henderson woman."

So much for my new-found "self." So much for conquering victimhood, for placing full confidence in my own measured, balanced view of myself.

Wrapped in wet towels, I got down on the floor next to Molly, who was still groggy from her anesthesia. If I wasn't dying of cancer—which I knew I *was*—then something had to be terribly wrong with my incision and I wouldn't be able to carry another child in my womb. Add to that a breast lump. Would I ever be able to nurse a baby? Was it Hamlet who said that troubles come "not as single spies, but in battalions." Whoever said it was right.

"And what about you, Molly?" I whispered. "Are you going to be all right?"

Molly looked at me with soft eyes the color of peat moss. Her dark blue pupils were tiny slits. She tried to focus on my face, but her lids kept lowering over her eyes, like a junkie's. She placed her paw on my arm. I rubbed it with my other hand.

"Don't die on me Molly," I whispered, pressing my face against hers. "Pleeeease, don't die."

The ultrasound showed a deep abscess in my incision, probably the result of trauma to the area. "Someday it will drain," my new OB-GYN, Alice Rothschild, told me. "But it won't kill you or keep you from having another baby." She laughed lightly and patted my hand. Although she took my concerns seriously, I could tell my hypochondria amused her. I didn't mind. I liked and trusted her.

Alice was my age and the mother of a young daughter. She came highly recommended, as did the two other young women in the practice, both mothers as well. Alice had long black hair and wore Birkenstock sandals over thick wool socks. She was definitely someone I felt comfortable talking to, even though she was a doctor. My breast lump, she suspected, was either a blocked milk duct or fibrocystic disease. She didn't think it was serious, but set up an appointment for me with a specialist.

The breast specialist, Dr. Susan Love, was another smart and sympathetic woman. She determined that I did have a blocked milk duct.

"You're not going to die," she reassured me. "And probably it's going to resolve itself, in time."

Maybe I could get pregnant after all — and soon. Despite the endless parade of disaster scenarios that marched through my mind — stillbirths, miscarriages, deformities — I was determined to be "with child."

Then Alice phoned with a new wrinkle. My blood work showed I wasn't immune to rubella, also known as German measles, a disease that, if contracted during pregnancy, could produce devastating birth defects. I needed to be vaccinated, she said, and then wait three months before trying to get pregnant.

"Three months!" I cried. "That's out of the question. We can't wait."

"You're going to have to," she said. It wasn't safe to start trying sooner; in the first three months, the antibodies from the vaccine could still be active and dangerous.

Three months seemed forever. Malcolm had only lived six weeks — forty-five days to be exact — and that brief time period loomed like a century. How was I supposed to wait three whole months? I was sick and tired of waiting, of living a life on hold. With each passing day, I felt I was getting farther and farther behind schedule. My biological clock was ticking double-time, trying to make up for my losses.

"This means you'll get pregnant during the summer," Bill said, trying to be upbeat. "At least it won't be flu season."

"But what if I miscarry or it takes months to conceive?"

"Try not to worry," Bill said. "I think you'll get pregnant easily enough. The genetic counselor thinks so too. Everything's going to work out fine."

But he didn't sound completely convinced, and his blue eyes looked lusterless. I knew he too dreaded another pregnancy and birth. But at least he was able to *voice* a positive attitude. That was more than I could do. Poor guy. Not only did he have his own grief and uncertainty to deal with, he also had to try to bolster my spirits. And that was a tall order. I was going to have to learn how to console myself, think good thoughts, be hopeful. But at the time optimism seemed utterly impossible.

I called my mother.

"Why are you in such a hurry?" Mother asked. "You need to rest before taxing your body and your spirit with another pregnancy."

That was my mother's solution to everything: rest. A bad haircut? "Go lie down for a while, sweetheart." As if a stint in bed would magically replenish hacked off hair. Yet, this time I knew she was right, but I didn't want to hear it. I was desperate. Once I got pregnant, I told her, I'd still have to endure nine tortuous months of waiting. I was thirty years old. Time was running out. I had to get started.

I could have kicked myself for not getting the rubella vaccine the day Malcolm died. I hadn't known that I wasn't immune, of course, but I was still furious at myself for not seeking medical advice earlier. Waiting, I was convinced, would kill me. If I didn't die of cancer, I'd probably get run over by a truck or struck down by some other fatal condition. I felt like one of the death-obsessed neurotics Woody Allen often played in his movies.

Mother understood. Like me, she tended toward hysteria and morbid introspection. The classic hysteric isn't depressive or suicidal, but lives in anxious anticipation of the sudden end of her life, her precious life.

You could say that again. Every time I tried to take action, to make a phone call or a plan, it seemed another disaster was about to strike, sending me scurrying back under my rock. First it was Molly at death's door. Then it was me—I had lumps, needed vaccines. Now I had to wait.

I tore through several books searching for a helpful quote, I knew I had somewhere, about waiting. Finally, I found it in T. S. Eliot's *Four Quartets:*

I said to my soul, be still, and wait without hope
For hope would be hope for the wrong thing; wait
      without love
For love would be love of the wrong thing; there is yet
      faith
But the faith and the love and the hope are all in the
      waiting.

House Hunting

I was beginning to see myself as inherently unstable, see-sawing between manic joy and numbing despair. Daily, I broke appointments, too thin-skinned to go out and see people. Often I simply let the phone ring, for fear it would be someone who might set me off. I spent entire days dwelling on what age Malcolm would be and reliving our hospital days. I dreamt about him every night.

I had no idea where my new-found grittiness had gone or my obligation to myself to live my own life, to embrace what Malcolm never had a chance to know.

Bill suggested I call a realtor and go look at a few houses. "The Wakefield house is going to sell soon, and we'll want to start thinking about buying another one," he said. "It's that simple. So you should get to know what's available. It'll get you out and about a bit."

I could tell Bill was worried about me. I was worried too. I'd never been so reclusive, so passive, so stuck. I forced myself to call a broker and make an appointment.

For the outing, I shed my uniform of sweat pants and bulky torn wool shirt and dressed up in a wool skirt, tights, and turtleneck sweater. I wore my long, fitted wool coat and knee-high boots, not my usual lace-up hiking stompers. I knew the woman would ask me questions. I had rehearsed a simple script. We moved here from Rhode Island for my husband's work (that was the truth, in part). We were planning to buy something when the house in Rhode Island sold. I just hoped she wouldn't ask how long we had lived there. Only eight months? She'd be incredulous.

Of course, the one question I dreaded more than all others was "Do you have any children?" Mother had told me to just say "No," but that didn't seem right. It was a lie. Or was it?

The realtor's first and last question was: "What's your price range?" I told her. Instantly, her smile vanished and she lost all interest in me. I'm sure she felt she was wasting her time with me, and as it turned out, she was. She showed me a couple of bleak two-family houses. When we got back to her office, I left quickly, telling her I would call again. We both knew I wouldn't.

I decided to drive to Harvard Square. I hadn't been there since the night Malcolm died. I bought a cup of coffee at the Coffee Connection and sat watching the people pass by. My skirt felt itchy around the waist. The boots hurt my feet. Years earlier, I had spent hours in this cafe, dropping in with Katryna and other dancers after rehearsals. We had always dressed in comfortable leotards and sweats. I felt edgy and uncomfortable in my oh-so-proper clothes.

In the bygone days, a person in mourning wore black and was probably treated with deference; people were careful what they said in the presence of the bereaved. Little, if anything, was expected of them socially; they were rarely seen in public places and were criticized if they socialized too much — it was inappropriate. Drinking coffee in public cafes or house hunting would probably have been taboo. Some women even wore black veils. I understood why. I longed for one, a tangible buffer against the bustling world around me. I had read that in China mourners wore white and were given special canes to lean on because everyone knew the burden of grief was crippling. Mourners were expected to act crazy, out of their minds, for up to twenty-seven months. No allowances were made anymore for the bereaved. Death was an unacceptable subject — without rituals, rites, and behavior roles. At least that was my experience.

I could feel the familiar shroud of sadness descending like mist around me, but I forced myself to get up and walk to a stationer's store in the next block. I needed envelopes so I could start sending thank-you notes to the many people who had mailed gifts, thoughtful notes, and, in the end, memorial contributions to Children's Hospital. Some people had responded to every stage of Malcolm's brief life. Nurses had sent heartfelt Christmas greetings.

I decided to look for a book. Entering the bookstore, I almost bumped into a tall, smiling woman surrounded by an entourage of people, all admiring her Snugli-bound baby. I swallowed and walked past them. Life must go on, I told myself, even if I did feel perpetually on hold. But I had forgotten the name of the book I was searching for, along with author and subject matter. I wandered aimlessly up and down the store aisles, like a shoplifter, my heart beating rapidly and unevenly.

Frustrated, I left, knowing full well I would remember the title when I got home and be furious at myself for having drawn a blank in the store. On my way out, I passed the mother and baby again. Someone was asking her, "How old is she?"

"Four months," the mother said, flushing radiantly and stroking her baby.

That was exactly how old Malcolm would have been. Four months. I walked swiftly out the door and straight to my car. There was something else I had intended to do in Harvard Square, but I knew I couldn't do another thing. I climbed over a dirty snow drift in my slippery, useless dress boots, threw the car door open, plopped into the driver's seat, crossed my hands over the steering wheel, and buried my head in them.

The inside of the car was as cold as a freezer. I blew air onto my gloves trying to warm my frozen hands. Who was I trying to kid? None of my little projects, like house hunting and buying envelopes, could bring my baby back.

Stormy Weather

A blizzard raged. Bill and I were out shoveling one of the huge snow drifts that kept encasing the car. It was growing dark and the only other person braving the elements was Brian, the five-year-old boy who lived in the other side of our two-family house. While we tossed snow, he threw snowballs for Molly.

Brian often stopped by our apartment, wanting to pet Molly. He would sit on the couch, stroking her, and talk to me. No one from his large family next door seemed to care where he was or what he did. I would see him alone up on the avenue or in the laundromat at the corner, trying to jimmy change out of the coin machines. Sometimes when he visited, I offered him a snack, which he never refused. Greedily he shoved hunks of cheese or whatever else I could find into his mouth, until his chipmunkish cheeks were bursting.

Brian was my only regular visitor and he was easy to deal with. I could just say, "You have to go now, Brian. I'm busy." Even if he'd only been there five minutes, Brian would give Molly one last stroke on her back and scramble out the door. I could tell he was used to being chased away. I felt sorry for him. Sometimes when I heard his erratic kid-knock on the door, I would cringe with Molly upstairs in the bedroom, feeling unfit for human company, even that of a little boy who only wanted to pet my dog.

"Hey, Molly's shaking all over," Brian yelled to us now. "She's biting at the snow!"

The snow seemed to be falling and rising at the same time, the way it does in those little touristy snow globes you shake to create flurries. I could barely see Brian or Molly through the furiously swirling powder.

Bill and I called to her and dragged her upstairs to our apartment. Brian was right; she was shaking all over. Her gums were pale. I couldn't find pulses in her cold hind legs, her belly was swelling, and she was gulping air — the unmistakable symptoms of bloat. Standing over her from behind, I picked her up under her arm pits and jostled her ribs, hoping to force that pyloric valve open. She shook violently and escaped, lunging at stray carpet strings. Bill dialed the vet's number, but got put on hold before he could explain anything, and then was cut off altogether. At least someone was there. We would have

148

to venture out into the storm and get Molly over there. We knew we didn't have much time.

The vet's office was about fifteen blocks from our place. Bill drove carefully, inching the car down the avenue. I held Molly in my arms. She struggled against me, biting at the upholstery, then at my down jacket. Finally we were there. Mounds of snow filled all the parking places out front, so Bill just left the car in the road, hazard lights flashing. The receptionist told us Dr. Fuller was snowed in at home. She suggested we drive to a twenty-four-hour emergency clinic in a north-shore suburb called . . . Wakefield (oh, irony!). It was the only place open, she said, and gave us directions.

Dr. Fuller called in, and she began telling him about other clients.

"Excuse me!" Bill said, wildly waving his hands in front of her to get her attention. Dealing with Malcolm's emergencies had made him a pro at getting attention when we needed it. "Please call Wakefield and tell them we're coming — with an emergency case of bloat."

He carried Molly back to the car. She shook and gulped at the snow in the air. The wind howled around us and the snow blew in all directions, making huge white tornadoes and ever-taller drifts. We coaxed Molly into the back seat and I got in with her. I checked her gums — still gray and lifeless. She struggled to get away from me, but I held her and thought bleakly of Malcolm, the day before he died, when he had raged so uncontrollably. Now I couldn't calm Molly either. It was getting dark. When we passed under a street light, I could see the whites of her eyes. They looked like those of a stallion who has just stepped over a snake.

We passed dozens of abandoned cars littering the shoulders of the highway. Bill crept along in the right lane, at twenty-five miles an hour. Occasionally, some fool would skid by us in the fast lane, causing mounds of snow to slam against the windshield.

I thought about an emergency trip we had made to Rhode Island Hospital with Malcolm. The highway rotaries, treacherous in any weather, had been under eight inches of water. I felt like we were traveling the Inland Waterway in a motorboat. Passing trucks sprayed us with huge waves of rain; stalled cars lined the shoulder. Bill crept along in the right lane. I had sat in the back with Malcolm, the way I was now with Molly, watching him sweat and strain for breath.

The emergency area had looked like a Hieronymus Bosch vision of hell. Wide-mouthed babies were screaming. A man, bleeding from a wound to his face, moaned in a chair. A woman clutched her abdomen and rocked, her face chiseled by pain lines.

Bill checked in with the receptionist and I found the only empty chair. Luckily it was far from the other people and their diseases, but it was in a draft. Malcolm was fussy, so I nursed him.

"Excuse me," Bill said, to the receptionist. "Malcolm Henderson is a direct admission," a phrase Patty Romph had told us to use to circumvent the normal admissions procedures. "We need to go right to the PIC."

"I'm sorry," she said. "There are the standard pre-admit forms you need to fill out and some questions you need to answer."

Bill sighed. I tried to stay composed. Malcolm dry-heaved and grunted in my arms.

Meanwhile, a line of anxious people had formed behind Bill. He repeated to the receptionist that her questions were unnecessary. "Malcolm is a direct admission," he kept saying. With her head down, the woman straightened small piles of paper on her desk and seemed not to hear him. She gathered a sheet of paper from each pile, attached them with a paper clip, and handed them to Bill.

"Please have a seat and fill these out," she said, her voice monotonic. "Come back to the front of the line when you're finished."

"But you don't *get it!*" Bill yelled. "My son is a direct admission. They're expecting him. I was just on the phone with his doctor. I'm going to go find her right now."

He shoved the papers at the woman and stomped off.

A nurse rushed into the waiting room, almost bumping into Bill, and called out "Malcolm Henderson."

"He's a direct admission, June," she said to the receptionist. "I told you that. You should have sent them right back."

I hurried after her. The man behind us in line roared: "What's going on here? You've been making these people fill out forms that don't even apply, while my wife is hemorrhaging out in the car. My wife is *dying! Somebody* do *something!*"

As the nurse led us through the double doors into the depths of the hospital, I watched the receptionist grab a microphone: "Emergency assistance," she bellowed. "Emergency assistance."

The car swerved on ice, but Bill got it back under control. I clutched Molly and hid my face in her fur. Here we were again, desperately hoping to get to an ER in time. I would tell the folks at the front desk that Molly was a direct admission.

As we approached the Wakefield exit, Molly burped — a gigantic noisy belch — and immediately seemed to calm down. I took off my glove, reached for her cold hind leg, and thought I felt a pulse. I hugged her, and with all my energy willed her to survive.

Suddenly, she turned serene, as Malcolm had on his final morning, when he seemed to know instinctively that he was going to die and was resigned to it.

"Don't get any ideas, Molly," I said. "You are going to get better, hear me?"

She licked my hand. I squeezed her to me tighter. She licked me again, this dog who never licked. Maybe she was trying to thank me for all those walks. Maybe she was trying, before she died, to let me know she loved me.

"Live, Molly," I said, as a command, like "sit" or "stay."

She did. The vet told us that the belch had alleviated her symptoms, but that she could have another attack any time. He insisted on keeping her overnight for observation.

Entering our apartment without Molly there at the door to greet us was almost too much for me. I remembered entering the Wakefield house, childless. I couldn't bear the stillness, then or now. We would have to get another dog, a back-up dog.

Tasha

At a glorified commercial pound called Buddy Dog, I found her. Tasha was a small, white, poodle-terrier mix, who shared a cage with the last of her puppies. She seemed desperate to get away from the little thing, but had no-where in the cage to hide from its sharp puppy teeth. She looked up at me, barked, and wagged her stumpy tail. She didn't look happy. In fact, there was a pitiful look on her face, as if she were saying, "Please, get me out of here."

Her puppy was the ugliest dog I had ever seen. It was grayish white with a big black splat, like spilled tar, over one of its eyes. I guessed it had some Jack Russell terrier blood. Its coat had small patches of curly hair surrounded by straight stubble. For a tail, it had what looked like a chewed up stogie.

"Believe it or not, we won't have any trouble finding a home for the puppy," the woman in charge told me. "But with Tasha, it will be harder. People prefer younger dogs."

According to the woman, Tasha was about two years old, a friendly, housebroken dog who loved children. But her file showed that she had been at Buddy Dog once before. She had delivered at least two litters and had lived in at least two homes. The woman was vague when I asked why.

Once I got her home, I found out. She growled men-acingly at Brian, proved to be *not* housebroken, and was an insufferable garbage hound. Tasha returned from trips to the park with used bubble gum and discarded candy matted into her beard. When I cut the sticky mess out of her hair and whiskers, she always snapped at me.

Kafka wrote: "All knowledge, the totality of all questions and answers, is contained in the dog." It was true of Molly, but not Tasha.

I loved her anyway. How could I not? She weighed seven pounds, fourteen ounces, exactly Malcolm's weight at birth. I carried her around and hugged her. I bathed her, brushed her curly coat, and swaddled her in towels. I even considered offering her a bottle and dressing her in baby clothes, but stopped myself. As a small dog, the vet told me, Tasha was less likely to develop bloat. This meant I could bond with her — without fear of losing her.

But Tasha was jealous. All I had to do was touch Molly and Tasha would lunge at her, all teeth. She was a needy, greedy, soulless little creature who craved my undivided love and attention. I didn't blame her for that. She'd had a rough life. But when Molly went down in a play crouch, ready for a game, Tasha would only growl, snap, and re-treat under the couch. Molly looked at me and tipped her head as if to say. "Why the hell did you bring her home?"

Perhaps they would get along eventually. Meanwhile, I felt sorry for Molly and terribly guilty for having foisted Tasha on her.

Deja Vu

Within days of Tasha's arrival, Molly had another bloat attack. Bill called Dr. Fuller and we rushed her in, leaving Tasha at the apartment. For all her faults, Tasha was, at least, a living creature to come home to. Dr. Fuller knocked Molly out with anesthesia, clamped her mouth wide open with forceps, shoved a tube down her throat, and drained the air out of her belly.

It was rare to see bloat in such a young dog, the vet explained. As we listened to this man talk — about valves, the odds, and surgery — I looked over at Bill. His face was tight and he flinched at the doctor's words. Neither one of us could believe what we were hearing. More valve trouble, more dismal odds, more surgery.

There were no guarantees with the experimental new surgery the vet told us about, but at this point it was the only thing we could do to try to save her.

Two days later, Dr. Fuller operated on Molly. I spent the day on the living room couch, petting Tasha and waiting. For Tasha, it was a marvelous day. Except for a few interruptions from Bill, whom she growled at, she had me all to herself. Lacking empathy, she didn't sense my palpable anxiety the way Molly would have. Late in the afternoon Dr. Fuller finally called. The surgery had been successful, but he felt Molly was too weak to come home that night. We knew she must be pretty bad off because, as a rule, he didn't keep animals overnight.

The next morning, Bill and I went to fetch her. Dr. Fuller took us back to an operating area. Molly was lying on her side, groggy and weak. Dr. Fuller carried her to the car for us. At home, Bill carried her up the stairs into the apartment and laid her on a blanket on the living room floor. Her eyes were rolling in her head. She had a freshly shaved belly, with a long, red incision — puffy around the stitches — running up her middle. For us, it was a familiar sight.

"Is this some sort of perverse cosmic joke?" Bill said, looking down at our sick puppy. "First our baby, now our dog. If this were fiction, nobody would believe it."

That first afternoon Molly's temperature went up, not sky high, but two degrees above normal. She turned her head away when I tried to get her to drink some chicken broth, but I did get an aspirin down her throat.

All this attention to another dog was too much for Tasha. Watching me fuss over Molly, she growled, backed up on her haunches, and prepared to pounce. Molly simply looked at me with her melancholy, now-drugged eyes, as if to say, "Can you deal with this?"

"Tasha!" I said, a savage edge to my voice. "Stop that!"

Tasha snarled at me and disappeared under the couch. Every time I lay down by Molly, a low growl came from the direction of the couch. I wanted to throw a boot under there. Why had I ever brought this silly, ego-ridden beast home?

That night in bed I rolled away from Bill and let out a big, silent scream. It was a technique my mother-in-law had taught me — a way to relieve stress when you have to be quiet. I had done it countless times in hospital bathrooms. You tense up the muscles all over your body, scrunch your face into a tight scowl, and then silently shriek, releasing all the tension.

I crept downstairs to check on Molly. She looked thin and weak. Was she breathing hard or was I imagining it? Perhaps I was hearing Malcolm breathing. I took her temperature. It was still too high. I applied another hot compress to her belly.

In the morning, I banged pots and pans around in the kitchen, trying to interest Molly in eating or drinking. Before her surgery, any noise from the kitchen would have brought her running, hoping for a table scrap. But now she lay still and febrile on her blanket in the living room. She wasn't "coming around."

I called the vet.

"It might take her time to regain her strength," the doctor said, sounding slightly irritated. We suspected he was getting tired of our phone calls, perhaps wondering how we could be so overly obsessive about Molly's vital signs, which, from his point of view, were not so worrisome. But Bill and I realized we had absolutely no faith anymore in the healing powers of surgery.

I spend the night by her side, listening to her body sounds. Sometimes I think I hear Malcolm grunting, but it's Molly's uneven breathing. Every few hours, I slip a thermometer into her bottom. Her temperature is going down. At dawn, she seems more alert.

Slowly, Molly recovered, and the dogs became friends. Before long, the three of us were pounding through the woods together. Molly would chase squirrels one minute and rush back to check on me the next. Tasha was always hot on the trash trail. Regardless of whether I still needed a back-up dog—I had one now.

The Pacifier

I had to find something to do to earn some money, take my mind off myself, pass the time while I waited.

Women my age were supposed to be either employed outside the home or staying home with their children. Doing *something*. But with each passing day, I felt a thick, immobilizing fatigue spreading through my body. Going to the store to buy food exhausted me; making a phone call took an hour of preparation and my body shook throughout the conversation. How could I think of working at a job where I had to interact with people? I couldn't seem to do anything except walk the dogs and think about Malcolm.

Meanwhile, Bill was grabbing every writing job he could find. He was trying to scare up enough money to pay the rent on Willow Court, the mortgage and utilities on the Wakefield house, and still have savings left over for a down payment on a house somewhere around Boston. He was gone most days and often well into the night. He didn't object to my idleness; he told me he was confident that before long I would be able to concentrate and work again. I was just in a "tough phase."

A bright moment flared when our realtor thought he had a buyer for the Wakefield house. He stopped showing it and took the "for sale" sign down. At the eleventh hour, the bank didn't approve the buyer's mortgage and we were back where we started — stuck with the property, a financial black hole and, to me, a constant reminder of my failed past.

I had to find a way to lift some of the financial pressure off Bill's back. In our seven years of marriage, we had taken turns being the primary bread winner. When we were living in Los Angeles and he was learning the screenwriting trade, I supported us as a masseuse; when I first hit New York looking for dance work, he brought home the bacon writing corporate scripts. Now, with the drying up of my job, the full load was back on him. I sensed Bill would have been perfectly happy to rent a place indefinitely; he'd often said he could live in a motel room. But he knew how much owning another home and trying to have another child meant to me. So he was slaving to provide for us. On top of everything else, he was still trying to finish his novel. And here I was staring at the walls all day, doing absolutely nothing.

Instead of planning my days around job-hunting, I

spent shame-faced hours on our chilly porch, hiding behind the French windows, peering at the parents as they dropped off and picked up their kids at the church daycare center. Anna Quindlen wrote that, after her mother died, it was years before she could watch a mother and daughter out to lunch together and not want to strangle them both.

Finally, I took on a freelance writing assignment that I got through Bill. He had convinced the folks at Envision, a production company he sometimes wrote for, that I could handle the job, revealing that I had ghost-written production scripts for him before. Several Envision employees had made contributions to Children's Hospital in Malcolm's name; I suspected they felt sorry for me and were willing to give me a chance. So my future as a writer rested on my doing a good job with this one.

The task was to rewrite a script for Polaroid's annual stockholders' meeting, a huge affair coming up soon. I quickly discovered it was an assignment nobody else had wanted, for good reason. I reported to two arrogant and uncooperative male Polaroid marketing managers. As the date for the meeting got closer and closer, they would forget to send me the information I needed to finish the script, then yell at me for not having the rewrite ready. I would apologize profusely and then timidly remind them that I still needed certain figures and other information before I could finish the job.

I had no guts when it came to making demands on people, and my heart wasn't in this job. I wanted to care, and pretended to, but I felt like a complete fraud. Maintaining my cheerful persona, when underneath I felt desperately unhappy and empty, was a ruse I knew I couldn't keep up for long. The only good part was Ollie, the Envision producer I was working with—an eccentric, entertaining man who wore round, red-framed glasses and whose office was full of trinkets, toys, pink plastic flamingos, and bizarre pop-art objects.

At a script meeting, one of the Polaroid men had started bragging about his new baby son and passing pictures of him around the conference table.

"Those are cute," Ollie said, giving me a nervous glance. "But let's look at them later. We've got to finish the script review."

I wanted to hug him for that.

For the rest of the meeting, I thought about nothing but the dreaded baby photos and how much I didn't want to have to look at them. Luckily, the Polaroid guy forgot to bring the snapshots back out.

At last, with the stockholders' meeting only days away, the job was wrapping up. On my way to the final screening, I grabbed my raincoat from the hall closet instead of my heavy coat. I hadn't worn the raincoat since the fall. Heading into the conference room, I felt something in my pocket. I reached in and pulled out one of Malcolm's red pacifiers, still attached to a thin hospital washcloth. I shoved it back in my pocket.

"You're white as school paste," Ollie said, taking my arm. "Are you feeling all right? You realize I'll have to get you arrested if you throw up on my precious slides! Only kidding."

I didn't say anything. He kept looking at me, concerned.

"Really," he said. "Are you all right?"

"I'll be back in a minute."

I rushed to the ladies' room and locked myself into a stall — my old escape hatch. Sitting on the toilet, I dug in my pocket for the pacifier. My body was shaking, like one of those wind-up toys that gyrates in place. I put the pacifier to my nose and smelled it, recognizing Malcolm's sweet and sour scent. I wanted to scream and bang my fists against the wall.

I had to get myself under control; they were waiting for me back in the screening room. Desperate for a gesture that would move me forward, I suddenly slipped Malcolm's pacifier into my mouth, drawing my lips around it. I closed my eyes and sucked. Salivating, I pressed my tongue against the plastic and tried to bring back all the times Malcolm had been comforted by it — lying in his isolette, looking out the window of his room, leaving for the last time in the doctor's arms. I leaned against the stall wall and forced myself to recite a few lines of the Polaroid script.

Finally, I checked my hands. They were steady. I stood up, put the pacifier back in my pocket, and walked out of the stall. No one had come into the bathroom. I had no idea how long I had been in there. I splashed water on my face, wishing I had a bag of make-up so I could try to disguise my puffy red eyes and pale cheeks.

I took a final look in the mirror and leveled with myself. I would get through the day, but this would be the last official assignment I would take. Making money and trying to advance my so-called career would have to wait. I had other, more pressing, business to attend to. I took a deep breath, plastered on a phony smile, and opened the bathroom door.

On my way out, I tossed the pacifier into the trash then instantly regretted having done it. Was I daring to rid myself of that doleful object? Impossible. Suddenly I wanted to rip the top off the can, thrust my arm in, and pull the thing out again. I took a deep breath. Be brutally rational, I told myself. What if somebody came in and found me rummaging through the trash? "Let it go," I said in a harsh whisper and walked out the door.

Pandora's Box

An article on grief. . . . The author, a bereaved parent, recommends setting aside a special time of day to grieve. It can be the time when you scream and yell or go into the dead child's room and wear her sweatshirt, cuddle his toys, lie down on the bed and sob. Set a timer and when it rings, put everything away and try to turn your attention to other matters.

Everything relating to Malcolm is in the cardboard box from my mother's house, including all the letters we received. I will answer every one of them. For now, this is my job. And for me it's a full agenda. It's too bad if no one understands. I know what I have to do and I'm determined not to care what anyone thinks of this "work." No one even has to know what I'm doing. "I'm finishing a writing project, but I'm not ready to talk about it right now." That's what I can say, if anyone asks what I'm doing with myself.

I set the timer for one hour and opened the box. First, I organized the letters to follow the chronology of Malcolm's life. "Hooray, it's a baby boy, congrats!" went in one pile, along with the notes accompanying gifts. In another pile, I stacked the hopeful, concerned letters. Then came the notes expressing sorrow at his death. Letters from the hospital listing the donors to Malcolm's memorial fund came last. I planned to start with the early letters and work my way through the piles.

Before writing, I looked at Malcolm's pictures. I fingered his hospital wristbands as though they were worry beads. I studied his footprint on the birth certificate, tracing it with my finger. Once again, I regretted having pitched the pacifier and longed for a snippet of his hair. I read the list of people who had contributed to the Cardiac Fund; included were several doctors and nurses. I read a few notes from different piles:

Dear Bill and Carol,

I've been struggling for some time now to find just the right words to express the emotion and empathy I feel for and with you over the loss of little Malcolm — to eschew the cold clichés of public ritual, and the excesses and singularities of personal pathos and self-pity. I want to tell you in person, in private, to take strength from each other, to blame no one . . . take my example as proof that life does go on, and that from the ashes of disaster come miracles like my Jennie. You can have a miracle too, and you will.

Please accept the special love of someone who's been there.

Larry.

Dear Carol,

I regret not being able to reach you when Malcolm was ill and I knew you were suffering. . . .

I was glad that you were both able to hold and cherish Malcolm. Our first child, Sarah, died right before she was born and we never got to see or hold her. It was sixteen years ago, but Sarah is still in our hearts. . . .

Karen

Dear Carol and Bill,

. . . Once on Fire Island I saw an old boat washed up on the bay side. The boat had the words "Oublie Doux" painted on

163

the hull. Some French friends said these words meant "forget
gently."

Rod

Dear Mr. and Mrs. Henderson,
    The Children's Hospital Medical Center has received
several gifts in memory of your son, Malcolm. I am enclosing a
list of donors. . . . We hope you will derive some comfort from
the knowledge that these funds will continue to advance research in this area in a manner befitting future generations. . . .

I got out a piece of stationary and wrote the date at
the top: March 12, 1983. Malcolm had been dead four
months and one week. He would have been almost five
months and three weeks old. What would he look like?
What would he be doing right now? Rolling over? Sitting up alone? Would he still have that adorable peach
fuzz on his shoulders?

I picked up the first note, read it several times, and began composing my response.

For weeks I sifted my way through the notes, answering each one. Most days, when the timer sounded at the
end of the hour, I wiped my eyes and stopped writing,
sometimes in mid-sentence. I put everything back in the
box. My hope was that Malcolm's spirit — and all my feelings — would stay sealed up in that cardboard container,
until our next timed session together.

Some days, it worked.

A Glimmer

The sister of misfortune, Hope,
In the underdarkness dumb
Speaks joyful courage to your heart
The day denied will come.

Pushkin, "Arion"

Scrap of Paper

Walking slowly home with a few groceries, I saw Marty, our landlady, coming my way. Over the months, our lives had overlapped occasionally. She now had a golden retriever, and when she had to work long hours, I would take the dog out for her. Simon, her boyfriend, was Jewish, and they had invited us to a seder at her place. She was into co-counseling, or something like that, and when we ran into each other, she always seemed concerned about me. "How *are* you?" she would ask, gazing at me with sympathetic eyes, her head cocked to the side, the

165

way a dog does on hearing a high-pitched noise. I knew she had heard my wailing and pacing from her rooms directly below ours.

"You don't look so good," Marty said now. She was the forthright type. "Are you all right?"

I shrugged and didn't speak.

"Guess what?" she said.

"What?"

"There's a woman, a therapist right up Mass Ave in Arlington Heights at a place called Offspring. She specializes in counseling parents who have lost children." Marty gazed steadily at me. The crows feet at her temples pointed upward, giving her face a perpetually cheerful expression.

"Why don't you call her?" She paused a beat. "How about today?"

I tensed. "Oh, I couldn't do *that*."

"Why not?" Marty said. "It's a beautiful spring afternoon, perfect to make a phone call! Go home right now and do it."

She reached into her pocket and pulled out a scrap of paper with a name and number on it. So, I thought, this encounter had been preplanned. Marty had been watching for me from her living room window, ready to rush out when she saw me, on the pretense that she had an errand to run.

"Call her," Marty said, heading toward the avenue. Over her shoulder she added, "What the hell are you waiting for?"

What *was* I waiting for? I wondered, as I walked down the street toward home. Suddenly too tired to drag myself up the stairs to my dogs, I sat down on the outside steps and watched a group of preschoolers scribble with chalk on the asphalt outside the day-care center. I could no longer tell myself I was waiting to finish all my letters. I had mailed the last one weeks ago. Although I had no regrets about writing them — and sending them off had even brought a certain sense of business-like closure — I still felt uneasy and out of sorts, longing for a greater redemption that wouldn't come.

Nothing penetrated my dark, numb mood. On the outside, things were improving. My parents had shocked us by deciding to purchase the Wakefield house themselves, as an investment. Their plan was to rent it out during the academic year and use it for vacations over the summer. Bill and I had found a house in Arlington that we hoped to buy. Soon the rubella vaccine would no longer pose a risk to a fetus, and I'd be able to start trying to get pregnant. I should have been excited, energized by these possibilities. But I wasn't. Instead it was all gloom and foreboding, a heaviness around my chest and shoulders. Trouble appeared to lurk around every bend.

My dreams were becoming more upsetting. Almost every night now I heard Malcolm crying out for me from the next room. Wasn't grief supposed to abate with time? Why was I more reclusive now than I had been three months earlier? Why wasn't I feeling better?

Every day I felt Malcolm hovering around me, like an unappeased spirit. One day the radio had been playing a Motown tribute. Desperate for relief, I turned it up and sang along with the Supremes as I scrubbed the entire kitchen, floor to ceiling. When the floor dried, I danced frantically around the room to exorcise my dead son from the place, but nothing would make him go away.

I sat.

The church door opened and another group of children tumbled out, squealing and pointing at the bright-
colored scribbling on the blacktop. Where had I heard
other children squeal like that with joy? Suddenly, I remembered. It was at the Halloween party at Boston Children's Hospital. Orange balloons and black crepe paper
had hung from the nurses' station. When a ghost jumped
out from behind the desk and scared a demon, the older
children shrieked with delight. A clown — dressed in
bright polka dot pantaloons and wearing a purple wig
and a noisy red clown nose — honked at all the children.

Malcolm stared, wide-eyed, apprehensive, but interested. The nurses were enjoying themselves. They deserved every laugh they could get and so did the kids.
There was so little to laugh about in that place.

I told Cheryl (the clown) I was going to the hospital
cafeteria to get a bite to eat. She honked her clown nose
at me and did a little jig in her oversized shoes.

Forty-five minutes later, when I returned to the unit,
there was no trace of the festive Halloween atmosphere:
no balloons, no costumes, no shrieking, no fun. Cheryl,
dressed again in her nursing whites, was holding Malcolm.
Apparently, while I was gone, he had started fussing.

"What happened to the party?" I asked, taking Malcolm
from her and tucking him into my arms.

"The new baby from Florida died while you were gone,"
she said. "And the father was furious."

He had lambasted her for wearing a silly clown nose
and having a grin painted on her face, while his baby
was dying.

Cheryl bit her cheeks while telling me about it. I could
see she was fighting back tears. The father had told her

she was unprofessional. She covered her ears with her hands, pressing flat her curls, and shook her head. "Nobody's ever told me *that* before."

I told her I thought it was great that everyone had dressed up and tried to have a little fun. Yet part of me had been thinking how bitter, how bereft I would have been if Malcolm had died while I was in the cafeteria and I had come back and had to deal with a nurse dressed as Porky Pig.

Next door, a teacher opened the door and rang a little bell. The children shrieked and jumped up, pushing each other to be first in line. It must have been snack time.

I reached into my pocket and pulled out the piece of paper from Marty. In her schoolteacher cursive, she had written, "Cathy Romeo, Offspring" and a phone number.

I stared at the name and I felt a tingling sensation that started in my stomach and rose up into my head. It was a familiar feeling: Fear.

I didn't need to see a therapist. I was doing fine. Bill and I had been to a costume ball the week before and had danced until dawn. I spent a lot of time home alone thinking about the past, but I was keeping up with people, sort of. I saw my friends Tony and Harriet fairly regularly. They lived close to the park where I walked the dogs, and I often stopped by to visit them. I could talk to them about things. Harriet was one of the few people to have come to the hospital to visit Malcolm, and they too knew about loss. They were trying — so far without success — to conceive a baby. Every month, when the pregnancy test came back negative, they battled their own grief and loss. What could a grief counselor do for me, anyway?

I stood up and climbed the stairs, clutching Marty's piece of paper. When I walked into the apartment, the dogs burst into their frenzied greeting — Tasha yipping and running in tight little circles, Molly wagging her fanny so hard I thought her tail would snap off.

I leashed them for their walk, the day's highlight for all three of us. As we were heading out the door, the dogs yanking hard, I thought, What if I run into Marty on the avenue? She'll ask if I've called. But, so what? Who cares? I didn't need some hokey grief counselor. Basically, all things considered, I was all right.

But . . . was I really?

No. I wasn't. It struck me like lightning. I wasn't all right at all. I couldn't stand this existence one minute longer. All my life I had encouraged others to seek psychological help when they needed it. When I was first married, I had seen a Jungian analyst to help me grapple with disturbing dreams and trust issues. It had been enormously helpful. Why was I being so stubborn now? What *was* I waiting for — hell to freeze over?

I jerked the dogs back into the apartment and closed the door. They looked at me, aghast. Tasha began biting at Molly's ruff. Molly stood, her nose against the door molding, sniffing and whimpering, her tail low.

"Sorry girls," I said. "I don't want to do this either."

Determined, I unfolded the scrap of paper, picked up the phone, dialed the number, got an answering machine, and left a message for the counselor. I asked her to call me.

Cathy Romeo phoned that evening.

"How can I help you?" she asked, her voice clear, like the sound the rim of a crystal glass makes when you rub it.

Oh God, I thought, I'm going to lose it.

And I did. I sobbed like a tired toddler into the phone, unable to speak. Eventually she eked a bit of information out of me.

"I can't understand why I feel worse as time goes on," I said. "Shouldn't I be better by now?"

"For most people," she replied, "the hardest time is between six and nine months after the death."

I scheduled an appointment.

Witness

Offspring was headquartered in an old house. The waiting room, formerly a front parlor, was painted a soft peach color. The place looked homey, lived in, with handmade quilted pillows on the saggy couches and original watercolor landscapes on the walls. I sat down, wishing I were anywhere but here, and picked up a brochure about the place. Offspring offered infertility counseling and support groups for parents with living and dead children. There was also a day-care center of some kind on the premises.

"Carol?"

It was Cathy Romeo walking toward me. She had soft brown hair and droopy eyes, like a spaniel's. She looked a few years older than me, but like someone who had been immune to the turbulence of the 1960s. I imagined she was a church-goer, a casserole-maker, a proper woman with a clean house who ironed the family's sheets and, I noticed, her jeans.

"This way," she said, and touched me gently on the shoulder. I followed her upstairs and into a small room with violet walls.

"Have a seat," she said, closing the door. I looked around. Perched on every end table in the room was a box of tissues. I sat on the couch; she placed herself across the small room from me on a wing chair. The old building had crooked woodwork and doors that closed awkwardly in their frames. I could hear noises from other rooms and the sounds made me nervous. There was a raging torrent inside me and I was afraid the whole place was going to shake and crumble to rubble at my shrill lament.

"I'm glad you came," Cathy Romeo said.

"Me too," I lied, swallowing like a scared dog when the barometer drops before a thunderstorm. I feared there was no way this straight-laced woman was going to understand my raw emotions.

"Where should we start?" she asked.

I was dizzy and weak. But I opened my mouth and words began to pour out of me, a literal stream of consciousness. I described how I had felt, checking out of South County Hospital early and hobbling into my house before heading to Providence and Rhode Island Hospital. "I had come home without my baby," I said. "It felt so wrong. I didn't even know where Malcolm was."

I told her about how my neighbor had looked up from his lawnmower and then quickly looked down again. I knew he didn't want to talk to me, that he'd already heard the story from his wife, a nurse at the hospital — and the whole thing scared him. His response alarmed me.

I think I must have been raving or at least talking very loudly, but Cathy Romeo didn't seem to mind. Whenever I looked at her, her head bobbed up and down slightly, like a buoy at a boat mooring. "Go on," she seemed to be saying, without speaking.

It was as though Cathy and I were thumbing through a photo album and I was describing random pictures. These were the images that stalked me day and night. Maybe by telling her about them, I could make them go away, evaporate somehow. Maybe this was how Catholics felt when they went to confession. I had read somewhere that it was important for women to have other women serve as witnesses by listening to their life experiences. Maybe Cathy Romeo was going to be my witness.

I told her about the woman who beat her head on the floor and shrieked, *"Porque Dio? Yo quiero nada!"* I described the sounds the alarm made in the ICU and the panic that ensued. I told her about the terrifying ambulance ride I had taken with Malcolm to Boston, the day before his surgery. The whole way up, the nurse had joked and flirted with the assistant driver about her upcoming wedding. She had complained about having to work that day. Meanwhile, Malcolm, strapped down to a huge gurney, gagged and sweated. She ignored him. When I interrupted her to tell her Malcolm seemed cold, she glared at me, snapped opened a cupboard, pulled out a towel, and tossed it in my direction.

I told Cathy how much Malcolm reminded me of a wise old man and how that frightened me. I told her about Molly's episodes and how I was convinced death was stalking me.

I told her how ashamed I felt because I couldn't concentrate on work and couldn't make money. I had no career aspirations other than wanting to be a mother. I loathed myself for being so self-absorbed and self-conscious around people.

At one point I realized I was shrieking. I knew everyone at Offspring could hear me, but I couldn't stop. Cathy just sat there quietly. I half-expected her expression to fill with terror, the way the women's faces did in my dreams when I told them about Malcolm. But she looked back at me with an open, calm face. Her expression seemed to be saying "It's okay. Go on." She didn't cover her ears and yell "Stop!"

Eventually, I sank back against the couch, exhausted. There was still so much to tell her, but I was too drained to go on. I felt guilty, as though I had contaminated her apple-pie innocence, her purity, with my horror story. No one else had heard all these stories.

Cathy began to speak. She agreed with me, she said, that Malcolm must have had the spirit of a much older person, not a baby. She explained a theory of Elizabeth Kubler-Ross's about the four quadrants of childhood development: The first was called the "physical" and lasted from birth to one year; the second was "emotional," for ages one through six; the third, "intellectual," lasted up until adolescence; and the fourth, during the teen years, was "spiritual." She told me that sick children, even babies, often seemed to skip to the spiritual quadrant, bypassing the other developmental stages. They experienced heightened spiritual awareness, the way she sensed Malcolm had. She said she had no proof for this theory, but, having worked with terminally ill children, she knew it was true.

She talked about what happened when a parent died. Parents have given something, a legacy, to their children.

174

Of course, there is grief, but it's easier for the living child to find something to take away from the death of a parent than it is for a parent to find something to take away something from the death of their child—especially if that child is only a baby when he dies.

"So you feel as though you're left with a void," she said, "a deep, dark, cavernous hole that nothing can fill."

She told me she would try to help me find something to take back from Malcolm, something I could use to try to ease my pain. She talked about breathing exercises and something she called "visualization." I would summon Malcolm to me, tell him what I needed from him, let him offer it to me, and then let him go.

"What do you think?" she asked.

"I guess I need to try *something*," I said. But truthfully, I felt deeply skeptical and disappointed by her proposed remedies. What had I expected? Miracles, I suppose. Malcolm, returned to me in the flesh.

She told me that all my feelings were natural, even my desire to slaughter the women I saw out strolling with their babies. She told me I needed to honor all my feelings.

I bristled at her use of the word "honor." It was one of those New Age terms that rubbed me wrong. But I was desperate, willing to try almost anything beyond tying myself down to a railroad track. Visualization just might work for me; I had always been suggestible.

But we were out of time, and I would have to wait until the next session to get started.

I walked home feeling weak, but calm. There was something almost exhilarating about confiding in a complete stranger. Cathy was a specialist in the field, paid to listen to sad stories and seemingly impervious to their eerie power.

175

She had told me I could phone her anytime if I needed to talk.

But summoning Malcolm to me through visualizations? On the one hand, the process sounded thoroughly suspect — in the charlatan realm with auras and crystals. Not at all my kind of thing. On the other hand, Malcolm's spirit — whatever it was — did haunt me; I already lived with a constant vision of him in my mind. He was ubiquitous, breathing on me, filling up rooms with his cries. Maybe if I could relate to him in a new way, I would learn something, or as Cathy said, "Find peace in his company."

That night, when I told Bill about my session, he said, "It's true. Malcolm's with you all the time anyway. You even call out for him in your sleep sometimes."

"Is Malcolm with you all the time?" I asked. I knew he wasn't. It was a rhetorical question. We had talked several times about our different responses to Malcolm's death.

"No," he said, after a moment. "I think about him a lot, and I miss him, but he doesn't haunt me."

"You're lucky," I said, feeling a tinge of envy, soon overwhelmed by dread. "I don't know about all this visualization and communication. What if it doesn't work?"

"It's worth a try, isn't it?" Bill said. "And you're good at imaginative stuff."

"I guess I'll go back," I said, sighing. "Maybe it will make you feel better." I laughed half-heartedly.

"Well, to be perfectly honest," Bill said, "I *will* feel better if you go."

Something is upsetting me more than the thought of conjuring Malcolm up at will. It's the rest of what Cathy Romeo said. Once I received what I needed from Malcolm, she explained, I could then re-

*lease him and let him go, until next time. That's the part that makes
my neck ache and my head pound — the thought of letting him go.*

Healing Place

"Take a few minutes to concentrate on your breath," Cathy
said. "Send your breath right down to your feet. Let it
bring warmth and carry away tension and tightness. Allow your toes to uncurl, your ankles to relax. Move your
breath up your body. Let your inner organs and bones
feel replenished by oxygen, released from stress."

Cathy moved me through all my body parts, focusing
special attention on the scar on my uterus and the healing that was taking place there. She told me to imagine a
warm, golden light above my head, my own star. "Let its
healing light radiate through your entire body. Let it
cleanse you."

"Now pick a tranquil spot," she said. "A sanctuary where
you can meet with Malcolm."

A cold shiver ran down my spine. Voices from another
room leaked under the door. I heard the unsteady patter
of a young child's feet downstairs. Somewhere, someone
laughed. I didn't think I was going to be able to go through
with this exercise.

"The spot can be anywhere," she added. "Somewhere
you'd like to go."

My mind was blank. And then, suddenly, a setting appeared in my mind's eye. It was the field behind a house
on Cape Cod, where Bill and I had often spent time in
the summer as housesitters. A postcard had been made of
the view, and I had tacked one to the wall in the back

room where I wrote. A grassy tree-filled backyard was bounded by a low stone wall. Beyond, the wide meadow sloped down to a salt pond. Farther up toward the house and centered in the field, a lone cedar rose up, straight and regal, out of the tall, blond grass.

I placed myself at the top of the yard, looking out and away, toward the pond. I tried to smell the meadow — the dry sage sweetness mixed with the slightly briny odor from the salt pond. I tried to feel the gentle breeze, the soft air that rustled up from the pond, making the meadow grasses bend and wave. I imagined a warm day, a deep blue sky.

"Have you found a place?" Cathy asked.

"Yes."

"Now let Malcolm come to you," she said. I heard my pulse in my ears, felt sweat rolling down my bony ribs. I wanted to bolt. "Stick it out," I told myself. "What the hell do you have to lose?"

"Call Malcolm to you," Cathy said. "Be patient. Give him time to come to you, in whatever form he chooses. Be open to anything he might be trying to communicate to you."

I tried to imagine holding Malcolm in this beautiful setting. The only magnificent scenery we had ever experienced together was the view of the Japanese maple outside his bedroom window and one brief walk down the street.

I heard voices outside the room. Women were coming up the stairs. They were giggling. My concentration vanished and, with it, my faith in this exercise. The process seemed totally ridiculous. I wanted to get out of this stuffy place, run all the way home to my dark, safe morgue of an apartment.

Then, in an instant, I saw a woman standing out in the meadow, part way to the cedar tree. She had a young baby in her arms. It was me, holding Malcolm! Like a camera lens, I zoomed in on the woman with her baby. Just as I got close to her face, the image blurred. Before I knew it, I was standing in the meadow myself, looking down toward the ground. Malcolm, a toddler now, was in front of me, his chubby arms wrapped around my knee. He was looking up at me with his big, Mediterranean-blue marble eyes. That image faded and a new one appeared. I saw the two of us from the chest up. Malcolm was several inches taller than I. We were looking out at the view together, like two bronze reliefs, images on pennies. Our profiles were smooth and polished.

Suddenly, I was holding the baby Malcolm again in my arms. I could feel his warm weight. That image dissolved and was replaced by another, in which I was a few feet away, looking at myself, this mother with her young child hugging her leg.

"If you want, you can tell me what you're experiencing," Cathy said. As she spoke, the image of the two bronzed profiles loomed before me.

No, I didn't want to come back from my safe, sunny scene. I didn't want to lose these gentle pictures.

"You can take yourself to this place anytime," she said, as though she could read my mind. "It's all yours."

Eyes closed, I explained to her what I was seeing. "The only problem is that I can't seem to make him stay one age," I said. "He keeps skipping back and forth between babyhood and manhood."

Cathy suggested that Malcolm might be trying to tell me he had attained all he needed from life in his brief

179

stay with us here on Earth, that perhaps he had indeed traveled, spiritually, from infancy to manhood and then away. She wondered if there was anything I wanted to ask from Malcolm.

"I want to ask forgiveness from him," I said. "I want him to forgive me for not being able to protect him from his horrible life and from death. And I want you to forgive me, Malcolm, for not being with you every minute when you were in the hospitals. Sometimes late at night I know you cried for me and I wasn't there. I'll never forgive myself for that."

Linoleum floors, monitor screens, and fluorescent lights crowded in on my mind, usurping the pastoral view. I tried to get it back again, the meadow sanctuary. Squeezing my eyes tightly closed, I shook my head. For a moment, Malcolm came back. He was the grown bronzed man in profile, a young Adonis. I wanted him to speak, but he didn't.

Cathy asked me if I needed to forgive Malcolm for anything. I said no, I didn't need to forgive him for being sick and for dying, nor did I need to forgive the doctors and the nurses who had cared for him. All of them, Malcolm included, had fought for his life, and I was fully satisfied with their efforts.

"You can always write to Malcolm," Cathy suggested. "You can ask him questions in your journal. You can keep these images of him with you always. But for now, say good-bye, knowing you can meet him again whenever you need to."

I told him good-bye and opened my eyes, not yet aware of the enduring power those images would hold for me.

In my next session, Cathy recorded a relaxation tape for me to play at home.

"Breathe into the psoas muscle that wraps around your pelvis and make more room in your body. . . . Send breath into each vertebra and into your diaphragm. . . . Let your lungs expand. . . .

"Around your head is a glowing sphere of light. Call that to you and send it to your throat and allow it to feel more open. Imagine another sphere of light radiating around your chest. Let all these lights glow around your body as though they were a string of jewels.

"Maybe you're getting ready to come out of that time when your most basic animalistic parts turned you inward to bind your wounds — to be alone and to recover. Maybe you're ready and strong enough now to turn outward to the world again. . . . Ask yourself if you're ready to turn back to other people again, to give and to offer emotional support. . . . Draw in the strength to understand other people's failings, their inability to really understand or to offer you help in any way. Their own inadequacies paralyzed them so often, their own feelings of helplessness blocked them from reaching out to you, just as you felt unable to reach out to anyone yourself.

"Know that the only path to peace is through forgiveness — and so you can forgive yourself for any jealousy you feel for other people's good fortune. Just release those feelings, those tensions. Gradually, there will be more room in your life for bringing in new people and new feelings.

"You have had to revisit, again and again, the painful story of Malcolm's life. It is the only way to integrate the trauma into your life so that you can live with it, and then move beyond. You've been experiencing a form of post-traumatic stress disorder. Honor the process that is working slowly and gradually within you, allowing you to heal. . . .

"Whenever you're with Malcolm ask him if there is anything he wants to give to you. . . . Before he leaves you, try to offer him your blessing and to feel his blessing within you. Know that you can call him back whenever you need to feel him and then release him. . . . Imagine that your body is filled with light and blessed, and let that feeling stay within you always."

I went to see Cathy Romeo every week. At the end of one session, she told me she had been counseling two other women, both of whom had delivered stillborn babies. "Their experiences have been different from yours," she said. "But I think you might benefit from talking with them."

She gave me a piece of paper with their names and phone numbers on it.

More people to call! Taking the plunge with Cathy Romeo herself had been scary enough. Every time I was scheduled to see her, I came close to canceling. I'd always feel nauseous or have a sore throat on my walk up to her office. But I had done the things she suggested: I had written to Malcolm, visualized him, played the relaxation tape. At times I had felt relief, a kind of meditative comfort in the act of summoning my baby to me. Other times I thought it was pure bull, like believing in newspaper horoscopes. I didn't have Malcolm — never would — and that was the bald truth, no two ways about it.

Now, six months after his death, Cathy was suggesting I reach out and make contact with other women in my situation. Lydia's mom had suggested joining a grief group, and I had dismissed the idea as stupid — a sign of weakness. For me, grief would be my own private curse, all my problems were private curses. But I was sick and tired of my own noxious company.

I called the first woman on the list, Debby. She had lost her first child. The other woman, Dot, had older, living children. I wasn't ready for her yet.

"I've been wanting to call you," Debby said. "But Cathy Romeo wouldn't give out your number."

"Well, you can have it now," I said.

Grief Group

When Debby got out of the car for our lunch date and I saw her clearly, I realized I knew her! She and I had studied at the same dance studio six years earlier. Immediately, I calmed down. We could always talk about dancing if the other stuff was too painful. Since the days we had seen each other, we had both changed our last names. When I quit dancing I took on Bill's name; she must have done the opposite — reverted to her maiden name. That's why we hadn't recognized each other when we talked on the phone.

"I was wondering what happened to you after you left Boston," Debby said, laughing. "Little did I know!"

She looked into my face with eyes as dark as raisins. I remembered those eyes. Now they were pleated underneath with shadows. She looked like she had been through hell. Her face was thin and drawn now; her thick dark hair had been chopped into a severe bowl cut. I hated to think how different I must have looked to her.

At first we talked about dancing. She told me she was starting to look around for other things to do besides teaching modern dance.

"It's such a hard life," she said. Debby had always taught dance. I had been a performer and had managed a dance studio.

"It was really tough going back to teaching after Joshua died," she added. I couldn't imagine how she had done it — how she had stood, grief-striken, in front of a group of staring women and conducted a class.

Debby updated me on several dancers from around the area. One was a local choreographer, Dorothy Hershkowitz. I had performed with her regularly when I lived in Boston. We had been close professionally and spent long late nights and weekends in tiring rehearsals.

"When I called to tell her about Joshua," Debby said, "Dorothy wept."

"I never even considered calling Dorothy about Malcolm," I said.

"Why not?"

"We had been out of touch for so long, I guess," I said. "And on some level, I've wanted to hide from people. Did you ever feel that way?"

"What do you mean?"

"Did you ever feel like your grief was so enormous and made you so insecure that you just wanted to disappear and have nothing to do with anyone?"

"Nope. Not me," Debby said. "I tell everybody. I talk about it constantly."

She told me that at a grocery store, she would admire a baby in a shopping cart and then turn to its mother and say, "Your baby is the same age as mine, only mine's dead!"

Telling people brought her relief, she explained.

"I can't stand for anyone not to know," she said. "It's such an important part of my life that I can't imagine anyone knowing me, even briefly, without knowing about Joshua." She chuckled loudly, an odd mannerism. Talking about the saddest of things, she laughed.

I told her there was another reason I didn't like to bring it up with people: I felt competitive with other women who were ahead of me in the baby-making business. I was always counting and comparing myself to others.

"I do that too," Debby said. "But I still need to talk to absolutely everybody about it, even my friends with babies."

She told me about the Jewish tradition of sitting shiveh. Following a death, you opened your house to all your friends and relatives and talked nonstop about the deceased. She and her husband had done that, invited everyone they knew over to their house right after Joshua died. All day long, she had cried and screamed with her friends and relatives.

I compared her experience to mine right after Malcolm died. Debby had lived for years in the same community. Bill and I were staying in a hotel in a city we no longer resided in. We barely knew anyone in the town of Wakefield and certainly didn't have close relationships with people there. I was reminded of our stiff WASP memorial service in Princeton and the reception afterward, where I was so completely buttoned up and stoical — and proud of myself for my behavior.

On one level, I envied Debby her openness and the proud candor with which she exposed her pain to everyone. Yet, it seemed unfair to subject random innocent people to the force of her grief. Shocking women on line in the supermarket might have been cathartic for Debby, but was it fair? And did it really make her feel better, deep down?

"Doesn't it make you feel better to be talking to me now?" Debby asked.

"I suppose so," I answered, dubiously.

We picked at the sandwiches and canned soup, both of us admitting we had miserable appetites. I realized that, unlike Debby, I had found no public arena in which I could express my feelings. A month earlier, I wouldn't even have been able to tolerate being around *her*. For me, feeling isolated and completely alone had been a miserable, but unavoidable, aspect of grief — my "dark night of the soul." But now? I sensed something in me was shifting.

"You're really like a wild animal out in the wilderness licking your wounds," Debby said, laughing. "You and I have responded so differently." She shook her head in disbelief and laughed again.

She was right; we had responded differently. But ultimately, I was starting to discover, grief was a great leveler. Debby and I had both "been there" in our own ways, and that was what counted.

We compared notes on the well-meaning but tactless remarks people came up with.

"The one that really gets me," Debby said, "is when I hear God loved my boy more than I did. Several people told me that."

I told her about a friend of ours, a childless bachelor, who said losing a child, "seems momentous at the time, but it's really like having one of your kids stay back a year in school. It's not a big deal, ultimately."

We both laughed caustically at that one.

I told her Malcolm's crying still woke me up at night and how I had tried, soon after he died, to tell a friend about that.

"As you can imagine — considering it was me — I was reluctant to mention anything," I said. Debby laughed. "But I thought I was going crazy and wanted some reassurance. And do you know what she said?"

Debby shook her head, knowing it was going to be bad.

"She said, 'You mean you're still thinking about *that?*' As if the possibility that I would still be thinking about my dead son three months after he died was totally preposterous."

I gnawed on my lip, just thinking about how I had smarted at the time.

"That really set me back," I added. "There was no way I could bring myself to tell her I thought about nothing *but* my dead son."

"Let's face it," she said. "We're never going to forget it, and our lives are never going to be the same again."

I nodded.

"I don't know about you, but I desperately want to get pregnant again," Debby said.

"Me too."

"But there's just one problem," Debby said. "Getting pregnant involves having sex! Joshua died in the birth canal. How am I ever supposed to experience any sexual pleasure?"

Her husband wanted to have sex a lot; it comforted him. She went along, but spent a lot of time during their lovemaking thinking about her son's grave. "Not the most erotic image," she said, with a laugh.

I realized I too associated sex with death and was relieved to find someone else willing to admit the connection. Debby let it all hang out.

"Let's just hope," Debby said, "that one of these days, we'll be sitting around like beached seals, pregnant and complaining about how fat we're getting."

A week later, Debby picked me up and we drove over to Dot's house in a well-to-do suburb north of Boston. Dot was a fundamentalist Christian, a homemaker who smocked her daughter's dresses and spent a good part of every day baking. She was also a La Leche League volunteer and made home visits — at all hours of the night — to women who were having trouble breast feeding their babies.

"In a way, having other children makes it worse," Dot explained in her soft voice, as she served us herbal tea and homemade muffins at her kitchen table. She was tall, with dark brown hair and regular features. There was a gentle calmness around her. She had beautiful pale skin, with cheeks that blushed delicately when she spoke. "My girls were so upset about it and I've been too bereft to comfort them the way a mother should. On top of everything else, I also feel like I've failed them."

I looked across the table at the two women. The three of us couldn't have been more different. Debby was dark, sensual, fiery, blunt, and Jewish. Her candor was disarming, and she swore like a soldier. Then there was me, a pale-faced, repressed, blond WASP — a scrawny tomboy. I was an agnostic or, at best, a pantheist. Then Dot, sweet and soft-mannered, quietly devout, and defined by deep maternal instincts. Yet, despite our differences, we shared powerful common ground.

Even though Dot had three daughters, she talked about how alienated she felt from her friends who had children. "Right after we buried Carolyn, it started raining," she told us. "All I could think about was how Carolyn was going to get wet out there, buried in the ground. I got hysterical about it and wanted to go out and put a tarpaulin and a baby blanket on her grave. That's not exactly a topic you feel comfortable discussing with your PTA friends or the neighborhood moms."

Having other children made it even harder, she said, because she knew what she would be missing, to never have Carolyn.

The three of us talked about everything we shared — the inappropriate remarks of supposed friends, the jealousy we felt toward other women with their babies, our terrible fears about getting pregnant again, and our weird thoughts about where our babies were now. We knew we didn't have any answers for each other, but at least we were all asking the same questions and that was reassuring. I could tell them that Malcolm breathed in my ear and seemed to follow me around my apartment. They nodded. They understood. Even though their babies had never even drawn their first breaths, they could imagine what I was going through. We could discuss it all without feeling insane or morbid — without feeling judged. We knew, on some level, that we were all raving mad and that was okay. It was, as Cathy Romeo kept insisting, *normal*.

"I was trying for a home birth with Carolyn and I went into labor in my bedroom," Dot said. "I bled all over the carpet. Clearly things weren't going right and we had to go to the hospital." She explained that later she couldn't get the blood stain out of the rug, so she replaced the carpet. But when the men were leaving with the old one, she stopped them and insisted on cutting out a bloody fragment.

"They looked at me like I was nuts," she said. "But I couldn't help myself. I'll probably save that piece of carpet until I die. It's one of the only things I have from Carolyn."

Debby took me to visit Ingrid, a tall, strapping German woman, who was a friend of hers. Like Debby, Ingrid had birthed a stillborn baby. She was pregnant again and due in four months. We prodded her with questions, and she let Debby and me feel the baby kicking in her swollen belly.

To be pregnant again was terrifying, Ingrid told us. Her dreams were all mixed up; dead babies intermingled with live ones. There were conflicting scenarios, births and funerals, disappearances and rebirths.

"But what am I going to do?" Ingrid said. "I buried all my hopes with my baby, and I had nothing to live for. I just have to try to get through this."

Debby and I nodded. We could imagine how tough it was.

Ingrid told us her parents had come to visit from Germany and had gone to see their granddaughter's grave without telling her. Later, she overheard them talking about it.

"They wouldn't discuss it with me, though," Ingrid said. "When I asked them if they had gone, they lied and said, 'No.' They were such cowards. I needed to talk with them about it and they couldn't, wouldn't. As long as I live, I'll never forgive them."

One night, the phone rang.

"It's me, Dot," the voice said. She started to cry. I knew something must have triggered her and she needed to share her tears with someone who understood.

"Do you want to discuss it?" I asked.

"No," she said. "I just needed to call."

"Next time it'll be me calling you," I said.

The Innocent

The house we bought in Arlington had one great advantage: It was in pristine condition. After all the fix-up work we'd done on the Wakefield house, I never wanted to steam wallpaper off another wall or see the world through the haze of plaster dust ever again. This house was just fine. It had freshly painted white walls, shiny maple floors, new terra-cotta tile in the kitchen, and a nursery just like Malcolm's room — white walls with peach trim. We wouldn't have to do anything except weed the overgrown perennial beds that sloped in a jungly tangle away from the house out back. For some buyers, an untamed, steep backyard with broken stone steps would have been a drawback. The sellers had apologized for it, in fact. But, as my mother always said, a house only needs one buyer, one person to appreciate its idiosyncrasies. For me, a long-neglected garden was a definite plus. Rediscovering it and bringing it back to life would be a pleasure.

We had found the house through a "for sale by owner" ad in the newspaper classifieds. The young married couple selling the place had an adorable little boy, about a year old. When we went for a second look, Bill and the husband disappeared down the basement stairs to check out a repair, leaving me standing in the sparkling kitchen with the wife and her baby. She was trim and carefully made up, with perfectly cut hair, an ironed shirt, and neatly creased pants. I could tell she was an innocent: Nothing awful had ever happened to her. And she was determined to keep it that way. I imagined she would scrub clean her floors and her mind every day, vigorously trying to keep the tragic and the ugly out of her life.

She was holding her freshly bathed son tightly in her arms. "What are your plans for when you move in?" she asked.

"I just want to get pregnant again as soon as possible," I blurted out. "My first baby died."

Her eyes opened wide; her mouth formed into a tight, frightened little circle.

Instantly, I regretted my outburst. I tried to explain what had happened, then apologized for having mentioned it at all.

"I don't know what to say," she said, in a low, chilled tone.

"There's nothing to say," I answered and shrugged.

A year earlier, I too would have been paralyzed if someone had dropped that on me — their dead baby . . . wanting to get pregnant as soon as possible. Back then, I knew nothing about illness, tragedy, and death. I would have been horrified, repelled. I could see the abhorrence — and the fear — in her eyes. They were the eyes of an innocent.

Dot was right. You could tell immediately the people who had lost someone, the folks who understood in their hearts about grief. Dot had baby Carolyn to thank for turning her into a person who knew, a person who always now reached out to others who were grieving. Carolyn had taken away her fear of death, she said, and had given her the gift of empathy.

Quickly, the woman moved us out of her kitchen to show me the linen closet. It smelled of fabric softener. Every towel and sheet was perfectly ironed and folded. There was no blight on this house. If I ever had another child, I vowed to myself (even as I admired her housekeeping), I wouldn't shield it from tragedy. At some point, of course, I would tell the child about Malcolm, but not until I could talk about him calmly. I wouldn't want to burden my living child with the enormity of my own feelings about my dead son.

From the minute the men came back upstairs until Bill and I left, the woman stayed right beside her husband. When he invited Bill to look at a storage area upstairs, she went along, baby in tow. She wasn't about to be left alone with me again. I could hardly blame her.

I stood alone in the kitchen, looking out the window above the sink, and tried to imagine myself chopping fresh vegetables in this spot.

Somehow, it felt right. I went out on the deck overlooking the back garden. Phlox, day lilies, irises, and peonies were struggling for space among the weeds. I couldn't wait to get my hands into that dirt and start weeding. The first thing I'd plant would be rosemary, the herb of remembrance.

Stevens Terrace

We moved. Malcolm followed me to the new house. I knew he would. There was no escaping his spirit. Still, I was relieved to leave Willow Court, to get away from the church day-care center, the neon reflections from Massachusetts Avenue, the grimy walls and dusty smells, the pit out back, the scene of Molly's attacks, and the fierce emptiness that had flooded my heart in that house.

When we left, I promised Brian I would walk over with the dogs to visit him. Molly sat patiently while he hugged her and petted her head with his sticky hands. Molly was one of Brian's only friends.

It was our third move in one year. After this, I never wanted to relocate again. Tasha, our "bon-bon" dog, immediately parked herself on a couch pillow in the new living room. She too had been dislocated more times than she wanted to remember.

I gave Molly a house tour. Every other time I had visited the new place, the weather had been dark and rainy. Now, afternoon light streamed through the dining room windows. I noticed a vine growing up a trellis and over the deck out back — wisteria, one of my favorites. A row of lilacs in the side yard was ready to burst into bloom.

There was a loud knock at the front door. Bill was in the cellar and couldn't hear it. Tasha barked and cowered on the couch, but she didn't dare give up her spot. She looked at me with terror in her button eyes. I could tell she thought it was someone from Buddy Dog, coming to take her away.

With Molly at my side, I opened the front door to a tableau of smiling faces, a human group sculpture that could have been entitled, "Fecundity." Mothers, with children straddling their hips and clinging to their necks, stood on my stoop and smiled at me.

"Welcome to Stevens Terrace," said one mother, handing me a loaf of bread, still warm from the oven. I felt my cheeks beginning to burn. I had to say something, anything, but my throat slammed closed, like a chimney flu. The silence was broken only by Tasha's low growl from the living room.

Bill came up behind me. He must have sensed my distress from all the way down in the basement.

"Thanks everybody," he said, with strained friendliness.

I'm sure many of these folks had watched as the movers unloaded the truck, looking for clues about our tastes and the size of our family. I would have been curious too, if I'd been one of them. This was a tiny street, a cul-de-sac, with no traffic and few distractions. Perfect for kids, the previous owner had told Bill. We had heard that everybody on the block had children and was congenial. Wonderful, but I knew they would soon start asking questions: "We saw all the baby stuff. Where are the kids?"

I had told the movers to shove the baby gear into a crawl space in the attic and had busied myself with other tasks while they hauled it in. I was convinced that looking at it would bring bad luck, like a groom seeing his bride in her wedding dress before the ceremony.

"We're kind of busy right now," Bill said. "I'm sure you can imagine."

The women smiled and nodded. The children stared at us. No one moved. Did they want to come inside?

Debby would have invited them in, but I didn't. I couldn't. There was no way I could face those people, those sweet mothers with their children draped over them like Spanish moss, those women who could kiss their babies goodnight and know it was only until morning.

"You truly are weird!" Debby said, when I told her about the neighbors' visit.

"I felt terrible," I said. "They had been so nice, bringing me fresh bread. I knew they wanted to come in or for me to come out in the yard—or do something."

"It's all that WASPy stuff of yours about being in control at every moment. Why the hell are you so secretive? You could have told them everything. It would have been okay."

"But I would have cried and made a fool of myself, and in front of all those children."

"So what?" Debby said. "What's so terrible about that?"

Debby was lucky. She could get through tough moments without breaking down or feeling crazy. Under duress, she laughed; I sobbed. My "water came easy," as the Caribbeans said about people who cried easily.

"So you would have shown them around the house, bounced their babies on your knee, and shocked them with your sad tale," I said. "And you would have been laughing the whole time."

"That's exactly right," she said, with a loud cackle. "And I'd have a whole block of new friends by now. But here you are alone, stuck with all your secrets."

Someday, I promised myself, I would let the neighbors in.

Our new house was in walking distance of the same park I had traipsed through with the dogs all winter. But to get there, I would have to run a gauntlet of the neighbors' houses — the Norman Rockwell yards crawling with children, the stoops full of chattering mothers. I missed the anonymity and urban feel of Willow Court. And the park was no longer empty, no longer my frigid, private domain. As the weather warmed up, more and more people had appeared. It was almost summer. There was nowhere left to hide, except in my back garden.

I look at the houses up and down the street and know they are bursting with the sounds and activities of babies and small children. Our house is so quiet, so sad. Today my heart aches for Malcolm. I want him in the flesh. Forget all this visualization and conjuring. What crap! He belongs here with us, crawling around, exploring our new home, pulling himself up by Molly's ruff. The fog has descended on my spirit; I'm wearing my shroud of grief and self-pity. I want to scream.

But I have to remember: I don't always dwell in this sadness. It will sweep over me and then it will pass. There is no button to push for relief from the pain, no panacea. Grief has its own life, its own timetable. But I can reach out to Malcolm's spirit and hold it. I can lead him to our private sanctuary where we can enjoy the lovely Cape Cod view together. I can always take him there and tell him how much I love him.

That night I dreamt I was walking by a lake with my mother and father. I was crying and moaning about how unfair life was, how unacceptable Malcolm's loss was to me. My parents watched me and shook their heads, not knowing what to say or do. My mother took my hand and I seemed to wake up. But it was a dream within a dream. In the next phase of the dream I was still asleep, in a bed in a strange place, all alone. I was looking down at my body from a vantage point above the head of the bed. A warm comforting light filled the room.

When at last I woke up for real, in my room in the house on Stevens Terrace, I wasn't surrounded by the shadowy dread that usually accompanied my waking from a dream about Malcolm. I felt refreshed, hopeful. It was a first.

Emerging

There is no harvest for the heart alone;
The seed of love must be
Eternally
Resown.

Anne Morrow Lindbergh, "Second Sowing"

The Test

I crept down the basement stairs, careful to keep the little vial upright and still. It was a sacred object, like a miniature decanter of communion wine or a voodoo potion. I set it down on a shelf of paint cans in a far corner of the basement, out of the light, and vowed I wouldn't peer at it before its time was up. Then I retreated, taking the winding cement steps two at a time.

In my study, I stared at the computer screen but couldn't concentrate. Twisting my hair again and again into a tight bun at the nape of my neck, I wondered about the portentous news that was growing in the dark, dank cellar. I set a timer and drank a cup of herbal tea. Finally, the ticking turned to buzzing. The wait was over.

I felt woozy walking back down the stairs and gripped the railing for support. Either way the test came out, the results were going to be staggering. I stopped at the double steel sink, stalling for time, and looked out the window. Even from here in the cellar, we had a postcard view of the Boston skyline. The city looked like a miniature design of children's blocks, tiny rectangles piercing the horizon. The day was so clear I could see the blue harbor beyond the city.

Over in the cobwebbed corner, my future awaited me. I walked across the space, weak-kneed, and gazed at the glass tube. An unmistakable, clear, dark ring shone in the little reflecting mirror under the tube, like the light encircling a fully eclipsed moon.

I was pregnant!

My knees gave out and I sank onto the muddy cellar floor. "Thank you, thank you," I whispered, my hands clasped in gratitude, not to a father-figure god I didn't believe in, but to a host of archetypal maternal figures. I begged for kindness from Demeter and Gaia, the Mother Earth goddesses; Artemis, the goddess of childbirth; Kali, the Hindu great mother of time, the mysterious goddess who created life — and took it away.

I went back upstairs and made a telephone call.

"Dot?" I asked. "The test was positive!"

It was my turn to cry.

Birthday Blues

Bill was away in Kentucky on Malcolm's birthday. He was working on a script for one of those twelve-screen, multi-image documentary extravaganzas, which were so popular at the time, and had to go to Louisville to complete the final draft.

Trying to reach out to friends and be sociable, I had invited a college friend, Candy, up from New York. I had seen little of her in recent years; as soon as she arrived, I knew her visit was a mistake. Cindy wanted to talk about our college friends and the old days. She didn't sense that I was a completely different person now, that Malcolm's life and death had transported me to another realm, that I could no longer relate to the person I had been back then.

Luckily, Candy overslept on the actual birthday. I woke up early, sweating from a nightmare.

Bill is coming home on a plane. It crashes. His spirit, a little leprechaun-like figure, visits me and whispers in my ear: "Aren't you going to come see my remains?" He laughs and disappears. I rush to the airport. At the gate, where Bill's plane is due, are lines of tied body bags behind a roped-off area. I plead with a flight attendant to let me look at my husband's body.

"No," she says. "Not allowed."

"But I have to see him," I say. "I never looked at my son's dead body and I will regret my decision for the rest of my life."

She looks at me and scowls. "Here, you can see this." She tosses a plastic bag at me. It feels like it has warm bread dough inside. "It's his spleen and his bladder. That's all I'm allowed to show you."

I throw myself on the floor.

Wandering around the house, I though about how different this morning should have been. I should have been baking a cake, setting out party hats, wrapping cardboard books and wooden puzzles, chilling a bottle of champagne for the grown-ups. The stillness in the house was stifling.

I left a note for Candy and took the dogs for a long walk in the woods. The air was dry and blustery, with a hint of smoky leaves. As I sat on a rock, feeling the heat on my back, I also sensed the cool air underneath.

I remembered every detail from a year ago. I had lain immobile in the hospital bed, while the nurse took my blood pressure every fifteen minutes and slipped one of those paper thermometers in my mouth. The staff treated me like an invalid, not a healthy woman about to have a baby. As the day wore on, my labor pains faded. At around seven o'clock in the evening, they decided to cut Malcolm out of me.

A raised sheet separated me from the operation. I felt tugs and jerks as they sliced and pulled, but nothing actually hurt my numbed body. Everyone in the operating room cheered when Malcolm scored a ten on the Apgar test.

My perfect son. . . .

A high wind tossed in the upper tree branches, shaking them vigorously. But down where I was, the air wasn't moving. I climbed a maple and tried to feel the breeze. Tasha kept jumping straight up into the air, whining, and looking up at me with desperate eyes. I tossed a dog biscuit far away from the tree to distract her so I could think in peace and quiet.

Late that first night, when I was back from the recovery room, Bill had brought Malcolm to me. I held him and tried to get him to nurse. He had taken a few sucks at the breast and fallen asleep.

The next morning I lucked into a private room, maybe because I was the only mother on the ward who had requested "rooming in" — having my baby stay with me all the time. In the afternoon, Bill walked Molly down to the hospital. I waited at our window with Malcolm in my arms. "There's your puppy!" I said to him. I whistled, with two fingers in my mouth, a call Molly and Bill knew. I banged on the sealed pane. Bill turned Molly's head up toward our window and she wagged her tail. I don't know if she actually saw us.

At dawn on that fateful Saturday morning, a nurse had helped me give Malcolm a sponge bath in a plastic tub. I washed his fuzz-covered shoulders and squeezed water from the cloth over his head. I dabbed his strawberry blond hair with baby shampoo and massaged his scalp. He closed his eyes.

Later, we had walked down the corridor and stopped in front of one of the long windows. Our view was of a community baseball field and the sailboats and yachts at the marina farther on. We could see a fog barreling in from the sea, swallowing everything in sight.

Now, watching my dogs play around the base of the tree, I hugged its cool, smooth bark and tried to focus my thoughts on the baby growing inside me. But I knew that, from Malcolm's birthday until the anniversary of his death on November 5, I was going to relive every day-to-day detail of my first baby's brief and wretched life.

Maybe, when I got past the death date and could no longer say, "This time last year Malcolm was, . . ." maybe then I would start looking to the future instead of the past. It was Faulkner who said something like, "The past isn't dead; it isn't even past."

I lowered myself down from the tree and threw a stick for Molly. Candy would probably be wondering what had happened to me. What would I say about why I had taken so long on my walk? I wouldn't tell her the truth about my life, that I thought of Malcolm constantly, that today was his birthday. I wouldn't even tell her I was pregnant, not yet. Debby would laugh at my compulsion for privacy, but that was just the way I was. I was sick and tired of living such a secluded life, haunted by scary dreams. But I wasn't yet ready to broadcast my inner life, even to a friend.

"Recite a poem," I told myself. "Language soothes."

"'Stone' by Charles Simic," I said aloud.

"Go inside a stone. That would be my way. Let somebody else become a dove, or gnash with a tiger's tooth. I am happy to be a stone. . . ."

Tasha looked up at me, barked, and wagged her tail. "You like that one," I said. "Maybe you aren't such a trashy dog, after all."

Reciting poems to dogs had its rewards, but I couldn't help but think how much more satisfying it would be to recite poetry to a baby who was strapped into a pack on my back, pulling my hair and learning, by listening, how to make human sounds.

Still, I was grateful for the companionship of dogs, the next best thing to babies.

It's a Girl!

Dream: The mucous plug comes out. Feeling mildly crampy, I go into the bathroom and deliver three tiny fetuses into the toilet, all with pulsing heart sacs outside their bodies. I scoop them out and lay them on a towel on the floor. They look like tiny plastic figures, trolls with-

out hair. I dab at them with cotton balls to dry them off and talk to them in the most soothing voice I can find. One by one the hearts stop and the figures begin to shrivel up, like dead worms on a hot sidewalk. I don't know what to do with them. Should I flush them down the toilet, bury them, or burn them and save their ashes?

Bill and I sat in the doctor's office, waiting. They were going to perform a special ultrasound on this baby's heart, looking for trouble. I worried that this new baby was going to be psychologically, if not physically, marred from floating in a womb that I sensed was full of tears.

A nurse led us into a small room with some big machinery in it. I undressed and put on the hospital gown. A lab coat came in, introduced himself, rubbed something cool, like Vaseline, on my belly, and began tracing my abdomen with a gadget that reminded me of Bill's electric razor.

"Is that the heart?" Bill asked, pointing to something on the screen beside the table I was lying on.

"That's it," the doctor said.

I couldn't keep myself from peeking at the screen. I watched the little blips of muscle action and counted the rapid beats. I knew so much — too much — about babies' hearts.

"I'm going to take a few pictures," the doctor said.

"How does everything look?" Bill asked.

"Looks normal to me," the doctor said, although he seemed to be staring awfully hard at the screen. I hoped that didn't mean he was seeing something he didn't like.

I had read in my pregnancy books that the baby's heart had begun beating at four weeks. By three months, the major organs had already developed. Now, the bones were growing furiously, and the fetus had shed its primal ape hair that grew on the soles of its feet and the palms of its hands. Between the seventh and ninth month, the baby's weight was supposed to triple, that is, if all went well.

I let out a loud sigh. There was so much they couldn't see in those pictures. Patty Romph had told me she didn't think an ultrasound would have shown Malcolm's problems. But now, at least, we all could see two miniature arms and two legs. The baby's head, the doctor reported, was the right size.

"See there," the doctor said, pointing to the screen. "That's one of the clearest pictures I've seen in some time. This baby is definitely a girl, a very active and, I'm sure, *healthy* girl!"

Wise Old Man

I had to find a pediatrician. I knew how much difference a good doctor made. If Patty Romph hadn't been delayed leaving her island house that morning — if we'd been assigned the other pediatric cardiologist at Rhode Island Hospital, the brutal one — I'm not sure how we would have endured our ordeal there. And it was Patty who insisted on Dr. Casteneda; she had the clout to get him for us.

Bill had heard about a popular pediatric group in Cambridge and called. The receptionist told him we could schedule an interview with one of the doctors in the group but that we'd have to pay for it, like an appointment. For some reason, that policy angered us both, especially Bill. Couldn't we just meet a doctor for ten minutes to try to get a feel for him or her, without the meter running? What other profit-mongering policies did the group endorse? We didn't make an appointment.

Later that day I stopped to chat with Peg, an older woman on the block, who was sweeping her front walk. She was the mother of eight children and had a number of grandchildren.

"Feeling okay?" she asked. The word was out — everyone knew I was pregnant. And it showed.

"I got through the first trimester," I said. "That's a relief."

I asked her if she knew of a good pediatrician. Peg told me that all her children had been delivered and tended to through childhood by Dr. Weller, who had a practice in Arlington.

"He's getting old and crotchety," she said, "but he has a new, younger partner that everybody seems to like."

She looked at me and hesitated, as though she had something more to say but was uncertain about speaking up. I knew she knew about Malcolm. Soon after we had moved in, I saw to that.

En route to the park one of those first days, I had run into Marilyn, the woman who had handed me the warm bread when we arrived. She was sitting on her stoop with her two young kids. One lay on its stomach on the flagstone crying; the other was pounding the porch steps with a stick.

"It must be nice," she called out as I was passing by, "only having to worry about dogs." She grabbed a clump of her hair and pulled on it, showing me her exasperation.

"You're talking to the wrong person," I snapped, feeling instantly flustered and regretting my remark. "You don't know the half of it."

I decided I was starting to sound like Debby.

"Really?" Marilyn said, her nose wrinkling in confusion.

Trapped: I would have to explain to her *why* she was talking to the wrong person. So I told her, briefly, about Malcolm. Marilyn had taken it all in, then replied she had no doubt I'd be pregnant soon. "Everybody who moves to Stevens Terrace gets pregnant almost immediately," she said. "We've decided it's something in the water here."

"I hope you're right," I'd said. I smiled and started walking away.

"Hey," she called after me. "I know there isn't *really*, but . . . is there anything I can do for you?"

I shrugged and shook my head. The pity in her voice made me uneasy, weepy. A sympathetic tone of voice had always been one of my triggers. Up the street a few paces I halted suddenly and turned back to Marilyn.

"Yes," I said to her that day. There was something she could do for me. She could tell all the neighbors about Malcolm, so I wouldn't have to.

Now, here was Peg, the mother of eight, nodding slowly at me and saying, "I lost a baby too, you know. My second."

"I didn't know. I'm sorry."

"And I'm sorry for you."

"So, does it get easier?" I asked.

"Yes and no," Peg said. "You stop being so sensitive, but I still miss that child. And it was twenty-five years ago. Look at me! I'm crying — still!"

I thought of my grandmother's reaction to Malcolm's death. Her own first baby had died in infancy, more than sixty years earlier. As a child, I had taken it simply as family lore. When my baby had died, Grandmother broke down on the phone. "I'm crying for Carol and her baby," she had told Mother, "but I'm also crying for my own."

"People tell me I'm nuts," Peg continued, "because I have all these other kids. But I don't have *him*. No one understands that."

"I do," I said.

Peg smiled through her tears. She was a short woman with freckles and wavy reddish hair, a good Irish Catholic Arlingtonian. I wouldn't have wanted to discuss school bussing or abortion rights with her, but on this subject we were in alignment. She told me her infant son had been born and died in November. Everybody got mad at her that first Christmas, calling her a killjoy for crying and not wanting to be a part of things.

"The things people say to you, in the name of comfort!" Peg said, her mouth drooping at the corners. Her relatives had told her to snap out of it, to stop sulking, to cheer up. They told her she had some nerve thinking about a dead baby at Christmas time. He had only died a month earlier!

"I still cry about that dead baby at Christmas," Peg said.

"I'm sure you do," I whispered.

"And all that garbage about how God only gives you as much suffering as you can handle in life. What a crock! I'd prefer people say nothing at all than to hear that junk."

I knew Peg had more than enough to deal with in her life. Her husband was severely diabetic and about to lose a foot to the disease. Her grown children were struggling with various problems.

"Give those pediatricians a call," Peg said. "Dr. Weller is old now, but he's a good man and I'm sure he's gotten himself a fine replacement."

The receptionist told me I could just drop by that very afternoon to meet Dr. Weller's associate, Dr. Koretsky.

"You mean, for free?" I asked.

"Of course," she answered, sounding amused that I might think otherwise. She said Bill could come when he had time. "His visit will be free too!"

Driving to the office, I realized what an ideal location this would be. In warm weather, I could stroll the baby there. In an emergency, it was only five minutes by car. Strolling . . . emergency . . . every happy baby thought shadowed by a fear. Yet, I couldn't stop myself.

The receptionist told me Dr. Koretsky was busy, but that I could talk to Dr. Weller. "They cover for each other, so it's good to know both of them."

I didn't want to visit a surly old man, but I also didn't want to seem picky or demanding. So I said okay.

I entered Dr. Weller's office and sat down in a chair facing his desk. He *was* an old man, thin and white-haired. He looked up at me with piercing blue eyes. He had liver spots on his cheeks.

"Yes?" he said. "What can I do for you?"

Before I could speak, he surprised me by hopping up, like a lean young athlete, closing the door to his office, and nimbly sitting down again at his desk. My face must have signaled trouble, a road map of grief.

"What is it?" he asked, in a kind and fatherly voice, the sort of empathetic tone guaranteed to make me weep.

Next thing I knew, I was sobbing. I managed to tell

him that I was pregnant and that my first child had died. I got out a few words about my fears for this baby's health. I said simply that I couldn't imagine taking a healthy baby home from the hospital. Then I apologized for my behavior and told him I wasn't always like this — which only made me cry harder.

Dr. Weller listened carefully, his big, bony hands folding and refolding on his desk.

"First of all," he said, "you've been to hell and back and I can understand all your worries about this pregnancy. Nothing like this has ever happened to me personally, but I can appreciate what you've been through."

I felt the tears coming harder, but I knew in my bones I had found the right doctor.

He explained that he was slowing down, that his partner dealt with most of the new patients, that he didn't make hospital calls on weekends anymore to visit newborns. It would be Dr. Koretsky who came, if I delivered on a weekend.

"But all that aside," he said, "I'd be glad to be your pediatrician."

"Really?" I said, wondering why anyone would volunteer to deal with a crazy crybaby like me.

"Your reactions are perfectly normal," he said, reading my mind. "Try not to feel jinxed. You've had some bad breaks, but I'm confident this baby will be absolutely fine."

When I stood up to leave, he stood, too, and shook my hand.

"I look forward to caring for your new baby," he told me. I looked at the clock on his desk. I had been in there for thirty minutes.

"Thank you," I said. I wanted to hug him, but didn't dare.

"By the way," he said as I was leaving, "don't hesitate to call me any time between now and your due date. Taking care of babies also involves taking care of their mothers."

On my way out, I met Dr. Koretsky in the hall and introduced myself. I was composed, lucid, and full of wonder at the free-wheeling, unpredictable spirit of grief.

As I left the building, I hugged my tummy and tried to imagine walking out that same door in a few months with a sturdy infant in my arms.

Bathing-Capped Buddies

"Is this your first?"

I turned my head to look at the woman beside me. We were in a room full of women, all of us lying on our backs on mats, our swollen bellies forming a chain of rounded foothills across the wooden floor. This was the introduction to a series of prenatal exercise classes.

Is this your first? How was she to know that her question was the one I most dreaded? She had a broad, eager face with limpid blue eyes and a complexion like buttermilk. Not a single wrinkle marred her cheeks.

How could I tell this woman with the freshness of a Mary Cassatt painting that, no, it wasn't my first baby, that my first baby had died in a hospital full of screaming, terminally ill infants and raw-nosed parents? I couldn't just nod or shrug, a smile on my face. How could I tell her that having babies wasn't always the glorious celebratory experience our instructor was describing? Why should I?

Looking at this woman's shining skin, I knew without asking that this was *her* first baby. I felt that peculiar heaviness pouring through my body, the way a cloud shadow skulks across a sunny mountain, turning it suddenly dark and ominous. I was an evil presence in this cheerful room, a pariah. I didn't belong here. I couldn't stay. I had to get out immediately, before the first class was over, before I started screaming.

Smiling weakly, I looked at the floor and didn't answer the question. Maybe she would think I was a foreigner who didn't speak English. I might as well have been a foreigner in this exercise class. From the minute I walked in and overheard the other women chattering about labor coaches, cotton versus disposable diapers, and the stenciled baby bureaus on sale at Bed Works, I knew it wasn't the right place for me.

I stood, rolled up my mat, returned it to the corner, and walked out of the classroom.

Outside, a cold wind blew trash and dry leaves across the avenue and dust into my eyes. The Arlington bus was toiling up the wide road. I could easily have bounded across the street and caught it, but I decided to walk the three miles home. I didn't want to be confined, squished into a plastic seat, surrounded by germy, human breath.

The frigid winter air burned my exposed cheeks and froze the hairs inside my nose. I walked swiftly, with long trail-blazing strides, and tried to picture calming endorphins flowing into my bloodstream, acting as a balm on my constricted vessels. My baby poked me in the ribs. She always woke up and knocked on me when I hiked. I wanted to convince myself that my response to the class had been perfectly reasonable and understandable — given my circumstances. But, huffing toward home in the blood-chilling wind, I still felt like a freak.

"How's Chlorine doing today?" asked Mary, looking up at my huge belly as she dangled her toes and fingers in the cool water. Mary was an older woman who looked like a wrinkled tortoise. She was one of my buddies in the water aerobics class at the Arlington Boy's and Girl's Club, where my classmates had already christened my baby "Chlorine."

"Is she kicking hard, like we're about to?"

"She's kicking up a storm," I said.

I loved this class. My enrollment in it had lowered the median age by a good fifteen years. Not one of the women had thought to ask me if I had other children. To them, it was obvious I didn't or I wouldn't be here. These women were from a bygone era. To their way of thinking, once a woman had a baby, she stopped taking classes and stayed home with her child. These "gals," as they called themselves, had raised their babies long before "Jazzercise" franchises and day-care centers began renting the basements of their churches, long before most women combined child-rearing with bread-winning, and long before anyone would dream of prying into a classmate's personal history. Maybe the uptight 1950s hadn't been so bad after all — in some respects.

"Let's get started with our jumping jacks, ladies!" shouted Betty, our instructor. Betty was bow-legged, sinewy, and pigeon-toed — a true jock. Her hair was closely cropped, her skin tan. Some people might go to Bermuda for sun in the winter; Betty went to a tanning parlor over on Mass Avenue.

"It's a lot more convenient," she had said. "And cheaper."

Betty reminded me of one of my high school gym teachers; she was devoutly patriotic, a real no-nonsense type of gal. Her hoarse military-style commands were a welcome contrast to the reverent and breathy lyricism of the prenatal teacher.

Inching into the chilly water, we all sent up a collective groan of protest.

"Come on in, gals," Betty yelled. "It's only water. It won't bite ya."

I looked around at the other women. I was the only one not wearing a bathing cap. The others wore either brightly colored caps that strapped under their chins or strapless, designer styles with shaggy petals that made their heads look like oversized dahlias bobbing up and down in the water. They all sported box-shaped, skirted swimsuits with bosom stays, linings, and zippers up the back. Even though I was of a different generation, I didn't feel a bit self-conscious. That was such a relief, such a change.

"Arms over heads for jumping jacks," Betty yelled.

Once we had warmed up, we clung to the side of the pool for our leg lifts. Then we jogged across the shallow end, the weight of the water making our thighs pump hard and our suits balloon with air.

I was due in six weeks. Mary asked Betty if she knew how to deliver a baby.

"I haven't got a clue," Betty said. "They knocked me out for all seven of mine. But I understand they deliver them underwater in Russia. Stay in shape, ladies. We all might have to help Chlorine out!"

Everybody laughed. I sensed that these women, although perhaps scandalized by the sight of my bulging — albeit suited — body, were tickled pink by the presence of a young, ripening "gal" among their ranks. They took

215

a motherly pride in me and my pregnancy. I knew they'd do anything they could to help me out, if I needed them. They were tough old birds, veterans of the Depression, wars, and years of motherhood. Their easy camaraderie was like a tonic.

After class, I had the pool to myself for twenty minutes before the next group came in. I swam lengths and repeated, as a mantra, the number of the lap I was swimming, "two, two, two, two, two, . . ." for the entire length of the pool. It was a good way to quiet my mind.

Sometimes, the meditation didn't work and the old familiar fears loomed up. Gliding through the water one morning, I wondered what would happen to me if I lost this baby. How could I ever again face an empty crib, a quiet house, my desperate raw loss, by bathing-capped buddies, the world?

For the next several laps, I forced myself to imagine the healing light Cathy Romeo always talked about. There was a star above my head radiating warm beams through my body. As I breathed, counted laps, and made my progress through the blue water, I pictured an iridescent wake fanning out behind me, full of hope and promise.

Split Allegiance

On a ritual stomp in the woods with my dogs, I reviewed the pertinent information. It was February 10, four weeks from my due date. Malcolm would have been almost seventeen months old.

The heavy snow, the dark day, and the bare creaking tree limbs brought back all the feelings from this time last year. I had paced these trails, round and round, hoping to ease the torture of unfulfilled need for my baby — the frantic desire to feel Malcolm's weight in my arms, to relish his lips tugging at my breast, to run my hands through his blond hair, to gaze into his clear blue eyes, to tell him things.

Everything was different this year and, yet, the same.

We had moved. Molly seemed healthy; she had no symptoms. I was pregnant. But Malcolm still accompanied me on these walks through the woods. Rarely did my son breathe in my ear anymore — the new baby had filled my body and my senses — but his spirit was everywhere around me. The dusk brought with it a fiery sunset, like the one on the night he had died. I heard the sounds of longing in the howl of the wind.

Nestling upside down in my womb, this baby was awake. She startled at the cold snaps of the tree limbs and shivered at the harsh grind of my boots on the packed snow. She kicked and hiccuped. I felt sorry for her, having to grow inside the circle of my ambivalence. I wanted her so much, but I also ached for Malcolm. And fear, sitting like a brick across my diaphragm, kept me from communing with this lively girl. She deserved more attention. When would I find the courage to talk to her, to set up her bedroom? When would I stop having such troubling, confused dreams?

I had called Cathy Romeo and told her that a steel door slammed shut in my heart when I tried to let myself feel joy and excitement at the thought of my new child. Cathy reminded me that the physiological bond was already strong between my baby and me. She encouraged me to feel how much my body had supported this child.

Not a minute went by that I wasn't nurturing her, Cathy said. That allegiance was solid, unstoppable.

"Think about your umbilical cord, steadily channeling blood and nutrients into your baby," she said.

Cathy suggested I actually write a letter to the new baby. So I did, in my journal, and carried a copy of it in my coat pocket.

Dear Daughter,

I have had many fears and much sorrow during your brief life inside me. I hope you haven't felt my pain and confusion. I have tried to find joy in your steady growth and boundless activity. I know you enjoyed that day during the January thaw when we sat on the park bench in the sun and I pulled my shirt up, exposing my pale belly to the warm rays. You were heated by the sun too. And you saw the sunlight. You stuck an elbow or a heel or a hand out below my ribs, and I held it, like a handle.

I know you share my love of the woods and all its spirits, because you are always alert and kicking on our walks. The woods are where I feel closest to you. That's one reason why I walk the woods every day, to feel you.

Forgive me for my reticence. I want so much to nurture you. But I am petrified. My heart is full of love and fear. I confuse myself. I consciously try not to think about you, and for this I am also sorry. I can't help myself. . . .

I crumpled the letter and shoved it back into my pocket. When was I going to address the baby by name? She had a name — Olivia — but I couldn't let myself call her by it.

Those wretched seven months I had waited before getting pregnant seemed interminable, at the time. I had felt a wild need to get pregnant again. Now, as I approached my due date, I realized I had rushed into it, unresolved.

Yet how could you ever "resolve" the death of a baby, the loss of all that potential? In any case, the decision had been made. I was pregnant. I stopped walking and kicked at the snow, wishing I didn't have to think so obsessively about these things. I longed to feel nothing but pure joy at the thought of the baby growing inside me. And I hoped I wouldn't be an overprotective, hysterical parent, if I ever got to be a parent.

Bill and I were clear about one thing: I was going to try for a VBAC, a vaginal birth after cesarean. We had gone back and forth endlessly about whether to attempt a natural delivery. At first, surgery had seemed the less risky option. Who could trust nature, left to its own devices, to behave? Not me. One of my obstetricians thought a repeat cesarean was the way to go. She told us we could schedule the birth and not have to worry about the baby being late. This comment fed an irrational fear that my due date would come and go and nothing would happen for weeks. Finally, my placenta would stop functioning and they would have to cut me open. Inside would be a wrinkled, dead creature with inch-long nails and hair all over its body.

Plus, there was the trauma of the birth canal and all that could go wrong there. The cord could strangle the baby on the way out. Debby had known her baby was dead in the birth canal, and, yet, she still had to push him out. Disaster scenarios like hers clung to my mind like barnacles to a dock post.

Alice, the doctor we both most respected in the group, told us she had reviewed every aspect of my delivery with Malcolm and was convinced it had been "asynclitism" —

the head turned at an angle — that kept Malcolm from advancing through the birth canal. It was also what had kept my labor from progressing.

"Couldn't it happen again?" I had asked.

"Yes," she said. "But at Beth Israel the nurses will have you up and walking and squatting, letting gravity do its work." She reminded me that the nurses at the small-town hospital in Rhode Island had kept me supine, "with a thermometer in your mouth!" She had laughed when I told her that.

There was no reason, Alice told us, to think this baby couldn't be delivered naturally. My uterus had healed, risk of uterine rupture was minuscule, and she thought I had a very good chance of having a successful vaginal delivery. She also pointed out that a VBAC would be much easier on me physically.

"Let's not forget what your body's been through lately," she said.

Bill and I didn't know what to do.

Then, in the thick of the debate, a friend had a baby. Bill and I called to congratulate the couple a few hours after their little girl had been delivered, vaginally.

"Ann is sleeping right now," the husband Peter had whispered to us on the phone. "And Kate is asleep on her stomach."

That did it. I knew from experience there was no way a woman could sleep at all after a cesarean, and with her baby on her *stomach*, five hours after having her belly sliced open. What a delicious possibility — delivery followed by sleep. Then and there, we decided to give nature a chance.

Bill and I opted out of the birthing classes offered at the hospital. Instead, we practiced on our own the breathing exercises we had learned before Malcolm's birth. We did tour the hospital unit with a group of expectant parents and squeezed each other's hand when we ogled the newborns in the nursery. When the others walked through the Special Care nursery, we stayed outside. I overheard the nurse explaining about fetal monitors and respirators. We could hear the beeping machinery.

"These noises give me the creeps," Bill said. "But it's going to be different this time. I just know it is."

I went to the ladies room.

Sitting in the trusty stall, I had a conference with our baby daughter. "Listen here, girl," I said. "You and I aren't going to spend a lot of time in hospitals. Understand? This hospital or any other. Do you get my meaning?"

I felt a hiccup, which I took to mean a thumbs-up. It was a deal.

A Room of Her Own

I was due in five days. Dr. Weller was on the phone, calling to see how I was feeling. I told him that my mother was coming in two days and that she would be a comfort to me.

"I'm glad to hear she's coming beforehand," he said. "Babies do arrive early sometimes. I assume you have everything ready."

"Well, not exactly," I said. "We haven't set up the baby's room yet."

"That doesn't seem fair," he said. "You're not giving this baby a chance. She deserves a room, doesn't she?"

"Yes, she does," I said.

"Well, if I were you, I'd go ahead and set up one for her. It'll be a lot easier now than later, when you bring her home from the hospital."

Suddenly, for the first time, I truly believed that I *would* bring this baby home from the hospital.

Dream: All the grandparents have come to visit. They discover several rooms in our cellar, including a potential apartment with a separate entrance, a bath, and a kitchen. I tell Mother it's a perfect space for a live-in babysitter. She gives me a scared look and doesn't speak. I know she's worried because I have my hopes up about this new baby and she doesn't want me to be devastated if things don't work out.

Bill and I find rooms full of supplies, toys, washing machines, and dryers. I can't believe we haven't seen all this space before, but I don't say anything to my parents. After all, it's my house and I'm supposed to know what's in it.

I woke up thinking about all those rooms we had discovered in my dream. In Tibet, the original home of the Dhali Lama, it is said that there is a magical castle containing one thousand rooms, one for every emotion and every desire of the heart. There are rooms devoted to sorrow and to joy. One room contains underground rivers, another star patterns for predicting the future. I knew I had to find space in my heart and in my mind to create a real room in my house for my daughter.

Bill and I retrieved all the baby things from storage. He scrubbed down the crib and washed the changing table. Molly and Tasha stood by, fascinated. They smelled each item intently. So did I. I buried my face in the sleepers and inhaled their musty, milky odors. A faint smell of Malcolm still lingered in them. With each passing day, these colorful stretchy suits had grown roomier and slacker on him, the less he had thrived.

I dumped the baby clothes, the sheets, and the cotton blankets into a wicker laundry basket, took them downstairs, and stuffed them into the washing machine. This was one job Mother wouldn't have to do when she arrived in the morning. When I heard the first cycle pouring cleansing water over everything, I had to wipe my eyes. I sat my big body down on the cellar steps and apologized to the new baby. After all, these clothes were for her now.

When the room was ready, Bill, Molly, and I stretched out on the floor and looked around. Tasha had retreated to her favorite spot on the living room couch, her short tail pressed hard against her bottom. She was anxious — things were changing again.

I called to the baby. "Olivia," I said. "Your room is ready and so are we. Olivia!" Molly looked at me with her sad eyes and cocked her head. It was a name she hadn't heard before. I said it again: "Olivia! This is your room!"

There was nothing wrong with this baby's heart, I told myself, or with mine.

"Precious"

A sharp pain woke me up. It was 1:00 A.M., March 10, my due date!

This wasn't a false alarm. Within three hours, Bill and I were on our way to meet Alice at Beth Israel Hospital.

223

Before leaving the house, I woke Mother to tell her we were going.

"I can't believe it—precisely on my due date!"

"I think it's a sign of good times ahead," Mother said bravely, trying to be the optimist. I hugged her and wanted to stay in the safety of her arms. The thought of going to a *hospital* made the hair on my arms stand up. But then a contraction, measuring high on the labor Richter scale, told me I had better get going—and fast. Mother preferred to stay home, she told us, but would get herself to the hospital in a taxi if we needed her.

"When you get here," Alice had told Bill on the phone, "I'm going to hand-pick your nurse."

Our nurse's name was Karen. She was calm and soft-spoken, with tidy brown hair that curled under at her shoulders. She looked like a friend of mine from elementary school named Linda Carroll. Linda had worn her hair in the same neat style. She always wore perfectly folded anklets and had plenty of sharp new pencils that she was willing to share.

Karen was exactly what I needed—a highly efficient and fastidious person, and she was kind. When she handed me two gowns to put on, she touched my hand gently. I noticed that her nails were filed and painted with shiny clear polish. She left me to change in private. Bill went off to buy a cup of coffee. I slipped into the gowns and saw my chart lying open on a counter by the bed. I peeked at it. A word was written across the top of the chart: "Precious."

When Karen returned, I asked her what the "precious" meant, thinking it had something to do with my mental state. "Precarious" would have been a better choice of words. She explained that "precious" is what they call a subsequent baby, when a woman has lost a child.

I sucked in my cheeks and bit them.

"Don't worry," Karen said. "We're going to take extra special care of you and your baby. Everything's going to be just fine. I know it is."

She smiled at me. Before I could cry or say anything, a huge contraction doubled me over in pain. Karen attached a fetal monitor to my belly. "It's just a precaution, so we can hear that the baby's doing well," she said.

Listening to the baby's rapid heartbeat made me weak and nauseous; the smells and sights of the hospital whirled unpleasantly through my head. Just putting on those gowns had brought back so many horrible memories — of scrubbing and suiting up to go see Malcolm in Intensive Care, trying to sleep on hospital cots, sweating in rocking chairs. I felt like I was slipping back in time, into a nightmare.

When Alice examined me, I was only two centimeters dilated, even after several hours of heavy and regular contractions and plenty of pacing — letting gravity do its thing.

It was all too familiar, just like the last time. The nurses were changing shifts and Karen was going home. I felt like weeping. Alice told me not to worry. She would get me the right nurse.

When Sheila, the new nurse, walked into the room, I wanted to hide under the bed. She was short and squat, like a fire hydrant, and had a tough, foot-soldier's face. She came in talking at me with the kind of voice you use when you've caught a dog misbehaving.

"Okay," she bellowed. "We've gotta get this labor happening. Up out of bed, girl, and start walking the halls again."

Sheila disconnected the fetal monitor and gruffly yanked me out of bed. There was an IV line in my arm in case I needed an emergency cesarean. This was mandated for VBACs, in case of uterine rupture.

Up and down the hall Bill and I walked. I pushed my IV pole and stopped every few minutes so I could cling to the railing when a breath-stopping contraction overwhelmed me. Without the railing, I would have collapsed on the floor.

Just like last time, I was having terrible back labor. Even between contractions my back ached. It meant the baby was facing the wrong direction in my pelvis, the hard part of her head pressing against my back instead of my more malleable front.

By midday my contractions had stopped altogether.

"This isn't going to work," I told Sheila, my voice cracking. I wanted to curl up in a ball and die. "It's just like last time."

"None of that talk out of you," Sheila said. "You've got a baby to deliver!"

"I'm going to leave you and your husband in this room alone," she said. "And I want him to stimulate your nipples as much as he can. Sometimes this gets labor going again."

She left the room, closing the door behind her.

Bill and I had to laugh. This part certainly was different from our last experience at South County Hospital, where they wouldn't let him near me — as though labor were an infectious disease. But nipple stimulation didn't work. Nor did pacing and squatting.

At 1:00 P.M. Alice came in and checked me again. I was still only three centimeters dilated.

"I think we'll try you on a very small dose of petocin," she said.

"But I thought petocin increased the risk of uterine rupture," I said, horrified. "Plus, they tried petocin last time and it didn't work."

"That was last time, this is this time," Alice said. "And I believe it's going to work." Sheila nodded in approval.

I had to lie down while they added the petocin into my IV mix. They put me back on the fetal monitor. I listened carefully to the baby's heart rate, desperately anxious about her reaction to the medication. What about my incision? It might rupture.

I began to panic. Maybe the cord was choking my baby. Why wouldn't the baby descend into the birth canal? Did she know something we didn't know? Did she know, as Malcolm had, that she couldn't survive outside the womb on her own heart?

Within minutes, the drug kicked in and labor started again. Soon I was contracting regularly and hard. After an hour, I had dilated to five centimeters.

"You're halfway there!" Sheila shouted. "Keep it up."

I had never dilated that far with Malcolm.

Alice stopped the petocin drip, but the labor continued to progress — with nonstop back pain. I lay on my side and first Sheila then Bill dug their powerful knuckles into my lower back. I moaned in pain.

"You're doing great," Sheila said. "When are you going to start yelling? That's when it gets real exciting."

I vaguely realized that the nurses changed shifts again, but Sheila told me she was staying.

227

"I'm going to be right here till the end," she said. "And it won't be long now."

Labor was so consuming I didn't have brain power left over for worrying. Alice checked me and said, "I think you're ready to start pushing."

They had to move me into an operating room, another post-cesarean precaution. I noted the fluorescent lights and metal tables, but was too preoccupied by then to get the jitters.

After about thirty minutes of pushing, Alice said, "I see a head and lots of dark hair!" In the birth canal, the baby turned and my back pain disappeared instantly.

"A few more pushes and she'll be here," Alice told me. Then, in a gush of stinging, warm fluid, Olivia was out. Sheila held her up. She wasn't screaming. Before I had a chance to panic about that, my daughter looked me right in the eyes, dead seriously, as if to say: "So that's what you look like, you nutty mom!" (Alice said later that she'd never seen a baby give its mother such a hard stare at birth.)

Alice handed Bill a pair of surgical scissors and let him cut the cord. Then they put Olivia in my arms. This baby had black curly hair, so different from Malcolm's wisps of strawberry blond. Olivia looked me in the eye again and then rooted around for my breast. "Enough already," she seemed to be saying. "I want my first meal!"

A staff pediatrician arrived. "She seems absolutely fine to me," the doctor said. I was relieved he hadn't used the word "perfect."

The only problem with Olivia arriving on her due date was that it happened to fall on a Friday. She came late in the afternoon, at 5:40, to be precise. The weekend had already started, and Dr. Weller had said he didn't make weekend hospital calls.

But at eight o'clock on Saturday morning, Dr. Weller walked into my hospital room.

"You came!" I said, delighted to see him.

"Well, yes," he said, rather grumpily, "I did."

He took Olivia and lay her on my bed. He bent her arms and legs, felt around on her head, pushed on her internal organs, and listened carefully to her lungs and heart. I watched his face for the slightest change — a wrinkle in his brow, a tiny loss of color, a blotch on his cheek.

"How is she?" I asked anxiously.

He told me she seemed fine, but, as a precaution, he was going to order extra blood work and some heart tests. I hated to hear this, but remembered all too well that it had taken three days to find Malcolm's problems. I wanted the bad news, right away.

A nurse came in to give me some information about breast feeding. She told me to start feeding Olivia every three hours and to let her cry if she wanted to eat more frequently.

"You'll get her on a schedule that way," she said. "And a schedule is extremely important." She explained that my nipples would crack if I let the baby nurse too frequently. If my nipples did crack, I could rub them with lanolin, which worked for some women. She would get me a sample tube.

Dr. Weller sat and held Olivia while the nurse talked on. By the time she had finished, my head was swimming with confusing information. When she had left the room, Dr. Weller handed Olivia back to me.

"Don't listen to a word that woman just said to you," he said. "If your baby's hungry, feed her. I don't care if it's every fifteen minutes."

He stood up to go and said good-bye.

In the doorway, he stopped and looked back at us.

"I've changed my mind about all those tests," he said. "I'm going to cancel them all. Olivia is ready to go home."

I couldn't believe they were going to let me take my baby out of there. There was nothing wrong with her and I was going to walk out of the hospital with Olivia in my arms!

But wait, maybe somebody had made a mistake. On our way out, a doctor would tap me on the shoulder and say, "I'm sorry, Mrs. Henderson, but your baby can't leave. We've found something wrong with her."

It was time to go. Bill had already gone to get the car. No one had whisked into my room to tell me I had to stay. I dressed and washed my face in the bathroom. Voices from the bathroom on the other side of the wall penetrated my wall.

"We're going to have to run some tests on your baby," I heard a nurse saying. "We just want to make sure there's nothing wrong with his heart."

"Oh," the new mother said, naively. "It won't take long, I hope."

I wanted to break through that wall, grab the new mother in my arms, and hug her. "You poor woman," I wanted to say. "Grab your baby and escape."

Then a completely crazy thought hit me: The nurse had the wrong room, the wrong baby — *it was really me and my baby she was looking for.* I dumped my things into my bag, grabbed Olivia, and rushed from the room. No one was going to stop us this time.

Our departure went off without a hitch. State law mandated that a nurse carry Olivia out the door, but once we were outside, she handed my baby to me.

I walked away, just like that!

With perfect timing, Bill drove up to the curb. The day before Olivia was born I had mustered up the courage to borrow a baby-size car seat from a neighbor. I had made my mother go pick it up. Also, I had told everyone, "No presents, please . . . until later, much later." Now, hands trembling, I strapped Olivia in for the trip home.

Bill and I didn't sleep a minute that first night. We sat up, listening to Olivia breathe, checking her color, feeling her pulse, counting her respirations. Bill called Dr. Weller three times.

"She seems to be grunting," he told the doctor one time. "Her color looks off," he said, on another call. But each time he hung up, it was with a shrug of relief. Dr. Weller had told him — and kept telling him — that everything sounded perfectly normal.

Normal.

Dream: I discover a packet of marigold seeds and run outdoors to plant them, even though it's still cold and wintry. Some of the seeds sprout and immediately begin to bloom. I am afraid the plants will freeze. How will I be able to protect them? I just will, I tell myself. For good luck, I throw wildflower seeds — lupine, poppies, purple loosestrife, goldenrod — all over the banks of a frozen stream by the house. They too will survive the cold. I just know they'll bloom.

Despite our fears, Olivia thrived. As the years passed, we learned, slowly, to relax.

Ashes

Every year it came on in the same way, like a slow flu. My neck ached, my mouth became tight, my lips pulled downward into a frown. When I blinked, the hollows behind my eyes felt dry, like burnt toast. A gloom, tinged with fear, hovered at the edge of my vision and inched closer, like an ominous mirage. For days, the dread built. It was as if my body, my cells, remembered. Finally, the actual day arrived, September 22, Malcolm's birthday.

This one would have been his third.

I lay in bed and let the bleak images break over me in waves. Like waves, there was no use trying to stop them. Malcolm's eyes — always. The bereaved mother pounding on her husband's chest. The last kiss. Memorizing his face. The funeral parlor.

What would he look like now? I wanted to know his thoughts on turning three. I longed to hear him talk. Running across the room, would he lumber awkwardly or would he already have his grandfather's sleek runner's gait? Would he be a hugging lap child or an unstoppable motion machine, like Olivia had turned out to be?

It was the cruelest day of the year.

Before Malcolm, I had loved the dramatic skies and high winds of fall, the air that could turn from tropical to chilly in one vivid hour. My birthday and wedding anniversary, four days apart in October, had resonated magically. Now they were usurped by other dates — Malcolm's dates. The sun's low angle, the fast-moving clouds, the dry rustle of fallen leaves brought remorse, not eager anticipation.

I rolled around in the bed, succumbing to a pillow-punching rage. Better to let it out. Holding back made my neck stiffen painfully and the lines of my face ache.

Bill was not in bed beside me. The house was quiet. Where was everyone? I got up and walked down the hall to Olivia's room. The bed was empty. I padded downstairs. No dogs greeted me.

There was a note on the kitchen counter. "We're at the park! 6:30. Love, Bill." Knowing this would be a tough day for me, he must have gotten up with Olivia, who always awoke, in full motion, at five o'clock, despite the blackened shades we had installed and the blankets we tacked over the shades each night. (Dr. Weller called Olivia our "lark.")

I put water on for coffee and drifted around the still rooms. The quiet in the house was rare; it upset me. I walked into the study and scanned the bookshelves. There it was, sitting in front of a row of paperback fiction titles, the little brass urn with "Malcolm" inscribed across its front. I almost never touched the thing. When visitors thought I wasn't looking, they would glance at it. Any day now, Olivia, a precocious eighteen month old, was going to point at the urn and say, "What's in there, Mama?"

And what would I tell her?

All of a sudden, in a flash of inspiration, I knew what I had to do and that today was the day to do it.

I pried open the urn with a penny. Inside was a little plastic bag of gray ashes, sealed with a twist-tie, the kind you'd use to secure a bag of apples at the supermarket. How pedestrian, I thought. The ashes were well pulverized, like the stuff under the andirons the day after a hearth fire. I opened the bag and smelled inside. The aroma was slightly smoky, but had no hint of burned hair or flesh. I pressed my finger into the ashes, collected a little heap on my fingertip, pulled my finger out, and examined the gray specks up close. There were a few bigger, extra pale bits among the cinders. Bones?

I held my finger up to the morning light streaming through the window. This ash had once been the flesh and blood of my son. Then — poof! Reverse alchemy. My gold had turned to ash. He was gone.

Finally, I did it. I licked my finger and swallowed. What else would a mother, *this* mother, do? The ashes tasted salty, like tears. I felt as though I were sampling a portion of myself from a reserve deep within me, a place never before discovered.

What was left in the little bag was about the size of the ground basil I had bought at the store the day before.

This was all that remained of my son.

I secured the twist-tie and carried the ashes to the kitchen. I dropped the little bag into a paper supermarket bag. The kettle whistled on the stove. I made coffee and sandwiches and put them in the paper bag, along with a few juice boxes.

I got dressed and went outside, carrying the empty urn. It was a windy gray Saturday. I dug a deep hole by the lilac bushes that divided the side and back yards. I dropped the urn into the hole and covered it with dirt. I never wanted to see the thing again. Without even asking him, I knew Bill didn't either.

Then I walked around to the front yard and studied, for the umpteenth time, the spot where I'd been planning a special garden.

When Bill, Olivia, and the dogs got home from the park, I took Bill aside and asked him how he felt about a day-trip to Rhode Island. He liked the idea.

"Hey Olivia," he said. "Want to go to the beach today? In Rhode Island?"

Olivia jumped up and down and ran to the hall closet to look for her bucket and shovel.

On our way, we stopped at a plant sale. I bought a Lamar's weeping carolinias hemlock. It was going to be a focal point in the garden I would plant out front, in memory of Malcolm.

We drove to Wakefield and went straight to the beach. A cool wind blew. Gray clouds scudded across the big bowl of sky. Swimming season was over. The beach was empty. Olivia wanted to go down to the water right away, so we all took off our shoes and socks. I grabbed the bag of ashes.

At the water's edge, I threw a clump of ash into the swirling foam.

"Me, me!" Olivia shouted. I gave her a pinch. She tossed it, like a handful of party glitter, over the gray water.

"Bye, bye ashes," I said, flicking more off my fingers. I gave the last small handful to Bill. He tossed it in.

"Bye, bye ashes," Bill and I said, in unison, our voices suddenly hoarse.

"More ashes!" Olivia shouted, holding out her small dimpled hand.

"The ashes are all gone," I told her, and held the bag upside down, so she could see for herself.

Olivia started to protest just as a breaker crashed around her feet, sending sprays of foam up the pant legs of her overalls. She squealed.

"Chase me!" she yelled. I stuffed the empty plastic bag into the pocket of my jeans. We all turned and ran, toddler-speed, toward the dunes, the swelling sea close at our heels.

Epilogue

When the pupil is ready, the teacher will come.

Buddhist saying

Years later, on a drizzly December morning, my neighbor Gail and I stood solemnly in my back yard. She placed a small bouquet of rosemary and the last mums from her garden on the freshly turned mound of earth. Molly, age ten, had died the day before.

"She was considerate right up to the end," Gail said.

It was true. We had not had to look on, helpless, as Molly became demented, incontinent, or gimpy with arthritis. She never did hard time in an Intensive Care Unit, attached to tubes and monitors. When she died, she was a lumpier, grayer version of her youthful self, but still reasonably fit.

And she spared us that torment every pet owner dreads: We didn't have to have her "put down" and be haunted, for years, by our decision.

Even in her death, Molly was gracious, quick about it. Sick on Sunday. An inconclusive trip to the vet on Tuesday. "Bring her back in a few days for blood work if she doesn't improve." Dead on Wednesday.

The morning she died, I had put our daughters on the school bus and taken Molly for our daily walk in the woods behind our house. I threw a stick for her. She ambled off the path, tail wagging, and gingerly sniffed out her prize. As always, she carried it proudly back to the house.

I thought Molly was getting better. After throwing a few tennis balls for her, I left her in the backyard to sun herself in her favorite spot.

Minutes later, I went out to check on her.

"Come on in, girl," I said, thinking she'd be ready for her morning nap in our bedroom. But now, Molly was lying flat on her side. She managed to pick her head up and look up at me with her doleful eyes. Then, instead of rising, she lay down again, her head on the ground. It was the first time in ten years she hadn't come when I'd called her.

I rushed to her, knelt down and cradled her head in my arms. She was breathing heavily, a line of foam forming on her black lips. I looked at her gums. They were gray, the color of death.

I yelled for Bill. "She's bad," I said. "She's dying."

"I'll call the vet," he said. "Maybe she's had a stroke." He rushed back into the house.

I sat cross-legged on the damp ground and gathered Molly's sixty-five pounds onto my lap. I stroked my favorite part of her, the shiny black fur around her shoulders.

"You're the best dog ever," I said. She looked me right in the eye—a wistful stare. I looked back, trying not to cry. She had always been there for me. Now it was my turn to be strong for her.

"It's okay," I said. "You can go." Molly turned her head away, and I felt the life shudder out of her.

I just sat there, I don't know how long, with my dead dog in my lap. I watched the squirrels, always reluctant when Molly was outside, dart across the yard with a new boldness. Already they knew.

Molly had been present for so much — the three moves in one year, the buying and selling of two houses, our move to North Carolina to live in the house Bill had grown up in. She was a stalwart playmate for our daughters, even through their tail-pulling toddler years. On sidewalks and beaches, through woods and fields, Molly and I had logged hundreds of miles together. More than any other living creature, Molly had been my companion in grief. As my mother later put it, "Molly was your best friend."

I was so grateful to be able to hold her while she died. If only we could all go this way — in the arms of a life-long friend, after a morning walk.

One death brings up all the others. I thought about Malcolm's. If only I could have held him like that while he died. I had a chance to hold his body in the hospital chapel afterward, but I had fled.

I hadn't known anything then about loss or grief. I was a novice, uninitiated. Back then, I wouldn't have wanted to hold him while he died. Even the thought of it would have repelled me.

How I had changed.

As I sat feeling Molly's heavy dead weight in my lap, I rescripted Malcolm's death, thought about how I might have handled it now, so many years later. I could have said to Dr. Casteneda, "No more." (I knew there was no real hope, even enthusiasm, for the second surgery. Everyone knew.) I could have told the doctors to unhook Malcolm from those useless machines and painful needles. I could have said, "I'm taking him home to die in peace."

At home, I would have bathed him, dressed him in a tiny outfit, and wrapped him in a blanket. I would have rocked him and sung to him and told him how much I loved him — until he died.

Now, I would do those things. Back then? I couldn't. I didn't know how. I lacked the ability even to imagine such actions.

Not visiting Malcolm's body was one of the most naive acts of my life. But, I had forgiven myself. Before I lost Malcolm, my mission had been to push away, to try to bury the dark, unconscious, scary aspects of life. After Malcolm died, I had no choice but to sink headfirst into the very wasteland I had tried desperately to sidestep. Yet, as one recovering drug addict has written, it is in that terrifying state of nothingness and loss that one often first sees the "dark face of wholeness."

What is life, after all, without death? Light without darkness? Joy without sorrow? Searching for a sanitized happiness was no longer my goal. Nor was coveting the lives of others.

The task was to seek meaning, to deepen my own inner experience, to live with gratitude in the present moment, and to try to be a beacon to others in need.

As I felt the dark ache of grief for Molly sweeping over me, I knew there was no way to avoid the pain. Even though she was only a dog, I knew I would spend years coming to terms with losing her. Grief, I know now, has its own mysterious timetable.

Bill and I dug a deep hole in the backyard, under a dogwood tree, near the spot where Bill's childhood dog Duff was buried, along with my sister Nancy's dog, Daisy, who had died when they were visiting us one Christmas. Tasha, our back-up dog, would not be buried in our yard. We had given her to a cousin in California who was going through a wrenching divorce and had fallen in love with her on a visit with us. In her new home, Tasha had no young children to snap at and no other dogs to compete with. Now, with Molly's death, we were dogless.

When the girls came home from school, I told them right away about Molly. Colette, who was six, put her arm around me and said: "Just think, Mama, now Malcolm can throw cloud balls for Molly to catch up in heaven." Olivia went to her room to grieve alone. Her mother's daughter, I thought.

When Olivia had turned five, Bill and I told her about Malcolm's brief life. She was old enough to ask the hard questions we had dreaded: Why did he have to die? Where was his spirit? Instead, she skipped away to open the door for the cat, who had appeared outside, as if on cue. Telling Olivia had been so much easier than I had anticipated.

But the next morning I found her slumped over a bowl of Cheerios at the breakfast table. She looked up at me and said, "Just because I never knew my brother, it doesn't mean I don't miss him. I wish he was sitting here beside me having breakfast."

For Olivia, the story of Malcolm had just begun.

Bill and I vowed our daughters wouldn't grow up shielded from death, as I had. They have seen the bodies of dead relatives, been to funerals, and talked freely to their parents about the meaning of life and death.

When Rosie, our pound mutt, was hit by a car, Bill and I took the girls and our other dog, Daphne, to the vet's office to hug her lifeless body and say our good-byes. Later, we drew pictures of Rosie and made a list of her most lovable qualities.

That night, the woman whose car had hit Rosie made a courageous surprise visit, bringing us flowers and a note expressing "my deep sympathy for your loss." A random stranger, she had not only stopped her car to inform us she had hit our dog, she also phoned the vet later to find out if Rosie had made it.

She is not an innocent, I said to myself. She was someone who had been there. I thought of all the condolence notes I hadn't written, all the suffering folks I had shunned, all the deaths I had shuddered at and turned my back on.

But that was before — before Malcolm.

Every year I am aware of Malcolm's birthday. I always wake up on September 22 thinking about him, missing him, wishing he were present. For ten years, I couldn't get through a single birthday without crying. Some fleeting moment would inevitably trigger me: a few phrases of melancholy classical music heard on the car radio, a lanky boy about the right age pedaling by the house on a bicycle, my mother's phone call just to let me know she too was thinking of Malcolm — even if we didn't mention him.

Several years after Malcolm's death, after we had moved away from Boston, I contacted the other grieving women I had met and asked them how their feelings had changed over the years. "You go shopping and find yourself looking at the clothes for your dead child's age group," Debby said. She now had two sons, close in age to my daughters. She added, "There's always a sense, somehow, that someone is missing." After Carolyn, Dot had had a healthy daughter: "I never know when it will hit me. At my oldest daughter's school graduation, I suddenly broke down. Carolyn would never graduate from anything."

We all agreed that the best thing we had done for ourselves was to seek out Cathy Romeo — and each other.

Do I think about Malcolm often? Yes, just about every day. Do I find myself conjuring up a phantom son: a boy, tall like Olivia, with piercing blue eyes like Colette's? Not often. But I keep track of the big events he's missing — going away to camp, becoming a teenager, graduating from middle school, getting his driver's license. I can't help myself. I am still a mother who counts. And I am still a mother who cries, when I least expect to.

It happened at the Driver's License Office the other day. Having just passed the eye test without my glasses, I was ecstatic. (Never mind that I'd had to ask the examiner if the hieroglyphs I was squinting at were letters or numbers.) The good news was that, when my glasses were lost, I'd still be able to drive legally. All I had to do now was get my picture taken and leave. The entire ordeal had taken less than twenty minutes. I wouldn't even be late to work!

"You're up next," the examiner said. "Right after I photograph this young man." I glanced at the boy — clad in jeans, a white T-shirt, and oversized basketball sneakers. He ran his fingers through his mop of disheveled, dirty-blond hair. His father gave him a proud clap on the back. The boy beamed up at the camera, triumphant. He was sixteen and getting his first license.

Something about that boy triggered everything. My mood plummeted. In a flash the everyday world shattered, and I entered another reality, a timeless zone of deep, frantic pain.

Malcolm would have turned sixteen this fall.

Pallid in front of the camera, I faked a smile for the driver's license examiner. This too will pass, I told myself . . . until next time.

Every summer we return to Rhode Island for vacation. Sometimes we stay in our old house in Wakefield. My parents now have retired there full-time. They've completely remodeled the upstairs. Malcolm's room has been merged with the adjoining bedroom and so no longer exists. But the red maple is still there, in full glory, out the window. Sometimes, I look out and remember everything vividly — the sleepless nights, Malcolm's grunting, my sweaty terror. Other times, what I'm seeing is only an elegant tree I'd like to climb.

At the beach on sparkling days, I sometimes stand by the ocean's edge, in the spot where we scattered Malcolm's ashes. I gaze out at the razor-line horizon. I feel the play of the cool waves around my feet, the salty mist on my face, and the sun on my body. I'm glad we chose to cast our son's ashes into that magnificent sea. At the water's edge, I close my eyes and wait for the enduring image to appear, the one Cathy Romeo helped me find. It materializes on the inside of my eyelids, the image of Malcolm and me looking out at the view together, our silhouettes etched like bronze pennies. As long as I am of clear mind, I will find peace in that picture. And as I grow older, the image becomes sweeter and stronger. The wrenching memories recede. Like old newsprint, they are fading, becoming harder to read.

Malcolm and I stand together, gazing at the tranquil view. Our silhouettes are strong—mother and son, together. Always. We are bathed in radiant light. And love.